# Human Destructiveness

# Human Destructiveness

## Anthony Storr

**BALLANTINE BOOKS**
*New York*

To Robert

Copyright © 1991 by Anthony Storr

All rights reserved under International and Pan-American Copyright
Conventions. Published in the United States by Ballantine Books, a di-
vision of Random House, Inc., New York, and distributed in Canada
by Random House of Canada Limited, Toronto.

This edition published by arrangement with Grove Weidenfeld, a di-
vision of Grove Press, Inc.

Library of Congress Catalog Card Number: 91-93092

ISBN: 0-345-37502-5

Cover art: "Screams of Children Come From Seagulls" © 1991 Willem
de Kooning/ARS, New York

Manufactured in the United States of America

First Ballantine Books Edition: July 1992

10  9  8  7  6  5  4  3  2  1

# Contents

# Preface

In 1989, Fred Jordan, then of Grove Weidenfeld, New York, suggested that I might like to update a short book of mine, *Human Destructiveness*, which was first published in 1972. I accepted willingly, believing that this would be a short assignment which I should easily complete in a few weeks. In the event, I found I had to rewrite so extensively that it took much longer than I had anticipated. What began as a revision turned into what is virtually a new book.

Since 1972, many things have altered, including psychiatric terminology, views on animal behavior, and ideas about the relation of childhood experience with adult behavior. I too have altered. The more I know, the less dogmatic I become, and the more I feel able to accept and learn from the ideas of others. I hope this conveys itself to the reader; and I also hope that this new exposition of the subject is better organized, better argued, and more readable than its predecessor.

My especial thanks go to Dr. Robert Barton, who pointed out my grosser errors in the field of animal behavior. Those that remain are my responsibility alone.

Joy Johannessen was an expert editor. Her emendations have improved the text in many places.

# Human Destructiveness

# 1

## The Nature of Human Aggression

THIS BOOK originated as one of a series of Studies in the Dynamics of Persecution and Extermination, sponsored by the Columbus Centre of the University of Sussex. My task was to examine the hypotheses of dynamic psychology as they related to human destructiveness; more particularly, to that form of human destructiveness which is directed toward the persecution and extermination of other human beings. In such an undertaking, the contribution of the psychotherapist is open to question. Human destructiveness on a large scale is more obviously the concern of the historian, the anthropologist, the sociologist, or the political scientist. Psychotherapists spend their days closeted in their offices, trying to understand and ameliorate the emotional problems of distressed individuals. Some of these individuals may have behaved destructively toward others or may be wrestling with impulses toward violence, but such preoccupations do not necessarily throw light on the reasons human beings go to war or massacre each other. In the heyday of psychoanalysis, some thirty years ago, psychoanalysts were so convinced that Freud had discovered the ultimate roots of human behavior that they did not hesitate to rush in where angels fear to tread and make ill-founded interpretations of social phenomena. Those days are over; and we are, I hope, less inclined to extrapolate from the study of a few neurotic individuals in our attempts to explain the destructiveness of groups or nations. We cannot assume that the forces which account for aggression between nation-states are the same as those which drive individuals. Even amongst anthropologists, there is still disagreement about whether preliterate societies are naturally warlike, naturally peaceful, or both.

I first became interested in problems of human destructiveness and cruelty toward the end of the Second World War. I am not alone amongst those of my generation in feeling that the original newsreels of Belsen and the other concentration camps constituted the most shocking experience to which we had ever been exposed: even more shocking than the photographs of Hiroshima and Nagasaki. Those concentration camp pictures profoundly altered my view of so-called civilized human nature. We were certainly familiar with torture and cruel punishments as part of history. We realized, at least theoretically, that there was no limit to man's capacity for cruelty to man. Yet in 1945 many of us naively supposed that the nations of Europe were well on the road to outlawing the grosser forms of cruelty. That the rulers of Germany had willfully instituted a policy through which millions of human beings would be subjected to starvation, humiliation, degradation, torture, and finally extermination came as an appalling revelation. To my mind, even the gas ovens were not so horrifying as the deliberate destruction of living personalities: the obliteration of everything which gave meaning and dignity to individual existence. The piles of naked corpses, dreadful as they were, were less ghastly than the vision of emaciated survivors, often covered with mud and feces, who had been made to appear subhuman and disgusting so that their tormentors should have fewer qualms about destroying them.

How could men and women be recruited to carry out such policies? The concentration camps required large numbers of guards of both sexes. It did not make sense to suppose that all these people were sociopaths or sadists. One had to accept that quite ordinary citizens of what had been one of the most cultured nations on earth could be persuaded, without too much difficulty and on an unprecedented scale, to treat their fellow citizens with barbarous cruelty.

I am by nature squeamish. Reading a good deal of the literature describing the concentration camps was painful. Still more disturbing was the thought that if ordinary Germans could be trained to behave in such repellent ways, so could any of us. Do impulses toward sadistic cruelty lurk in the depths of every human psyche? What conditions or methods of training facilitate the emergence of such impulses or convert average citizens into torturers? Although my interests have widened over the last twenty years, such questions still preoccupy me, and I do not pretend that I or anyone else has discovered all the answers to them.

In my original introduction of 1972, I drew attention to the dispute, current at the time and still under way, between those who maintain that human aggression is instinctive or innate and those who affirm that it is wholly learned or a reaction to frustration. I pointed out that as with so many disputes, part of the difficulty is semantic. That is, different authorities use the term "aggression" in different senses. Some reserve it for unprovoked assault intended to cause physical injury; to others it is the underpinning for almost any form of active striving. For a thorough discussion of the variety of ways in which the word "aggression" is used, the reader should turn to Gerda Siann's excellent book *Accounting for Aggression*, to which I am greatly indebted, in spite of, and because of, her informed criticism of my own writing on the subject.

Some writers limit the word "aggression" to behavior which is either violent or else so obviously competitive as to involve disadvantage to another person. Gerda Siann points out that most experimental psychologists use "aggression" only in this negative sense. Most laboratory workers in this field also repudiate the idea that aggression is in any way innate or instinctive, believing that aggressive behavior is invariably provoked by environmental stimuli. The "hydraulic model" of aggression as an innate drive which produces accumulated tension requiring periodic discharge is repudiated by all modern theorists. However, it does not follow that aggression is unconnected with innate behavior patterns. Indeed, all aspects of human behavior depend both upon innate factors and upon environmental influences, and authorities like Donald Hebb consider it meaningless to ask how much any given piece of behavior depends upon the one factor rather than the other.

It would avoid confusion if we were able to follow the experimental psychologists in confining the use of the word "aggression" to physical attacks or behavior obviously harmful to others. However, many psychiatrists and psychoanalysts concerned with understanding human beings as wholes rather than isolating particular aspects of their behavior find themselves unable to do this. For them, positive and negative features of aggression form a continuum. We should all like to rid ourselves of our proclivities for violence; but if we were able to do so, we might find that we could no longer stand up for ourselves or assert our separate identities. Aggression seems closely linked with self-preservation, self-assertion, and self-affirmation. An aggressive attack upon another individual involving the use of physical force is a crude, extreme example of self-assertion at the expense of the other. So are some attacks that involve only words. Anyone who has listened to a political debate knows that verbal exchanges can be remarkably aggressive, with one opponent accusing the other of dishonesty, stupidity, and malice whilst forcefully asserting the superiority of his own policies, abilities, and moral qualities.

Gerda Siann suggests that when someone uses the term "aggressive" to describe behavior, he or she believes that four conditions obtain.

1) The person carrying out that behaviour, the "aggressor," does so with intention.
2) The behaviour is taking place within an interpersonal situation which is characterized by an element of conflict or competition.
3) The person carrying out the behaviour in question intends by that behaviour to gain a greater advantage than the person being aggressed against.
4) The person carrying out the behaviour in question has either provoked the conflict or moved it on to a higher degree of intensity.[1]

The first condition is necessary because behavior which causes *unintentional* injury or distress cannot justly be labeled aggressive. If a child runs into the road under the wheels of my car, I may cause its death, but since I had no intention of killing or injuring the child, I cannot be accused of aggressive behavior.

The second condition appears acceptable at first reading, until one reflects upon certain kinds of behavior which must surely be called aggressive, but which do not take place within an interpersonal situation. A man trying unsuccessfully to unscrew the stuck lid of a jar may become so enraged that he swears at the offending object and throws it across the room. We may condemn such behavior as childish, but we can hardly fail to label it aggressive, although no other person is involved. Aggression can be directed at things as well as people. We are just beginning to take seriously the fact that our domination of the earth has become so destructive as to endanger the resources on which we depend.

Gerda Siann's third condition assumes interpersonal conflict and goes on to postulate that the aggressor, by his aggressive behavior, intends to gain some advantage over the person he is attacking. This seems to me questionable. Siann writes:

> Thus a child's desire for independence, as evidenced, say, by contradicting a parent, can be called "aggressive" by Storr, because he believes that parent-child relationships are characterized by conflict, and because he believes that the child wishes by his contradiction to gain mastery of the parent.[2]

I must have expressed myself very badly if this conclusion can be drawn from what I have written! Parent-child relationships, like other close relationships, are characterized both by loving cooperation and by conflict. The child who contradicts a parent may simply be asserting its own point of view rather than attempting to gain mastery as Siann suggests. When William Blake wrote, "Opposition is true friendship,"[3] he was underlining the point that close relationships invariably involve disagreement as well as agreement. In various

9

species of animals, parents may provoke conflict with their offspring before the latter are grown by partially rejecting them. Trivers has suggested that such rejection may benefit the parent by freeing the mother to produce new offspring rather than continuing to care for those already there.[4] Siann's fourth condition is acceptable.

In the last chapter of her book, Siann links aggression with the desire to achieve self-recognition and rightly affirms that a sense of devaluation fuels a great deal of aggressive behavior: "I would argue that, irrespective of culture, sub-culture or the era in which an individual lives, all human beings require a sense of personal significance and identity."[5] In Western societies, the majority of people who commit violent acts in peacetime come from the bottom of the heap, from those social strata in which many individuals feel humiliated, inadequate, ineffective, helpless, and of no account. The unemployed, the unskilled, the deprived, and the very poor do not easily accept their lowly status. Violence may be the only way such people think they can impress others or make themselves felt. Siann suggests that people who have been denied a sense of their own essential worth are likely to resort to violence as a habitual means of self-affirmation, and that the subculture in which they live is likely to reinforce this tendency by placing positive value on violent behavior. This is certainly the experience reported by a number of violent criminals. Siann quotes Jimmy Boyle, a former criminal raised in the slums of Glasgow, as saying that violence was the only way he knew of gaining a position. Here is another example.

Violence is in a way like bad language—something that a person like me's been brought up with, something I got used to very early on as part of the daily scene of childhood, you might say. I don't at all recoil from the idea, I don't have a sort of inborn dislike of the thing, like you do. As long as I can remember I've seen violence in use all around me—my mother hitting the children; my brothers and sisters all whacking one another, or other children; the man downstairs bashing his wife, and so on.[6]

The same habitually violent criminal makes a clear distinction between what Siann would call "instrumental" aggression and "hostile" aggression. Robert Allerton continued to have no scruples about hitting anyone who was carrying money or something he wanted, for violence in this context was simply part of the job. But as he grew older, he came to deplore "personal" violence; that is, he began to try to control the impulse to hit anyone with whom he was having an argument.

The environments described by Jimmy Boyle and Robert Allerton are urban rather than rural. This is hardly surprising; for it is surely in big cities that the individual is most likely to feel disregarded, to perceive himself as an insignificant cog in a vast machine which can easily dispense with him. In a village, hostile tensions between neighbors can be extreme; but individuals, even if disliked, at least are recognized. In cities, a person can remain almost anonymous for years and may come to feel that he counts for nothing.

It is clear that people who have been severely undervalued are likely to express their need for self-affirmation in violent ways because they perceive other people as rejecting or indifferent. Those who have received more recognition and who consequently have incorporated a greater sense of their own worth will be able to interact with others in a less hostile fashion. But everyone, however fortunate their childhood experience, continues to need self-affirmation. We all require recognition as individuals possessing separate identities.

In my admittedly broad use of the term, assertion of one's separate identity requires "aggression." Those who have been neglected and disparaged develop a particularly strong compensatory need to assert themselves, and so behave violently. Those who have been loved and praised have the same need but can affirm their individualities in ways which are not antisocial. If one accepts the fact that individuals need self-affirmation (and I agree with Siann that this is the case), then one must surely accept that there is a basic propensity toward self-realization, that is, toward expressing one's particular, peculiar, individual self. This seems to me as much part of self-preservation as protecting one's body from injury. One cannot assert difference from others without "aggression," however little that aggression may manifest itself in hostile or destructive ways.

In these pages, I am paying tribute to Gerda Siann's thoughtful book and agreeing with much of what she has written. But I am also disagreeing with, or attacking, some of her conclusions, and in doing so, I am asserting my own point of view and my own identity. If I thought that she totally despised what I had written or dismissed me as an idiot, my own need for recognition might prompt a more violent attack upon her point of view. How I respond is nevertheless a matter of degree and not of kind. Any disagreement, however mildly expressed, is slightly "aggressive," although, in this case, I hope that opposition is not incompatible with friendship. Here again the continuum between self-affirmation and opposition of a more forceful kind is evident.

Because self-affirmation varies in intensity from mild disagreement to murder, we cannot confine the term "aggression" to intentional injury of another or to exchanges which are personal rather than impersonal. Our use of language makes it plain that aggression must be interpreted in a wider context. We *attack* difficulties, and hope eventually to *defeat, overcome,* or *master* them. The intellect is often referred to as if it were a knife or other cutting instrument; for we *sharpen* our wits, *dissect* problems, and hope that our minds will retain a *keen edge.* Many aggressive metaphors appear to originate in Freud's primitive oral stage of development. We *get our teeth into* a subject and sometimes *bite off more than we can chew.* In arguments we may indulge in *biting* criticism or sarcasm. Abhorrent noises or other distasteful stimuli *set our teeth on edge.* Cheating is sometimes referred to as *biting,* and when the plan to cheat fails, the *biter* is *bit.* In *Romeo and Juliet,* to *bite one's thumb* at another is to offer a deliberate insult. *Biting one's lip* is indicative of suppressed chagrin or anger. Biting is linked with scratching in the phrase *tooth and nail,* which usually indicates intense striving. Even the tongue is included amongst our aggressive oral armory when we refer to verbal reproof as *tongue-lashing.*

Charles Rycroft, in his *Critical Dictionary of Psychoanalysis*, refers to the traditional meaning of aggression as "dynamism, self-assertiveness, expansiveness, drive," and points out that the word is originally derived from the Latin *ad-gradior*, which simply means "I move forward."[7] Other words derived from the same root are "egress," "regress," "progress," and "ingress," terms denoting movement outward, backward, forward, and inward. It might satisfy both experimentalists and psychoanalysts if we were able to confine the use of the word "aggression" to the way people behave when their self-assertiveness and expansiveness are obstructed or when their need for self-affirmation is repudiated. This usage would also suit those who believe that aggression is always the result of frustration. But we cannot do this. It is surely legitimate, as well as common practice, to refer to "aggressive salesmanship"; and an aggressive salesman may simply be promoting a new product rather than attempting to defeat rivals.

Even the exercise of aggression in war need not be accompanied by any personal animus toward the enemy, a fact which, in pre-nuclear days, may have partly accounted for the continued popularity of warfare. Today we can be thankful that most people are acutely and realistically aware of the horrors of war, but it was not always so. On October 24, 1914, the poet Julian Grenfell wrote to his mother:

> We've been fighting night and day—first rest today—for about four days. The worst of it is *no* sleep practically. I can't tell you how wonderful all our men were, going

straight for the first time into a fierce fire. They surpassed my utmost expectations. I've never been so fit or nearly so happy in my life before: I adore the fighting and the continual interest which compensates for every disadvantage. . . . I *adore* war. It is like a big picnic without the objectlessness of a picnic. I've never been so well or so happy.[8]

Julian Grenfell was wounded on May 14, 1915, and died on May 26.

In another book, Charles Rycroft writes that psychoanalysis "regards the self as a psychobiological entity which is always striving for self-realization and self-fulfillment. In other words, it regards mankind as sharing with the animal and plant world the intrinsic drive to create and recreate its own nature."[9] This drive is certainly assertive, and I think it legitimate to label it "aggressive," but I do so with regret, because I appreciate that others will think this usage unwarranted. Nonetheless, it seems to me more fruitful, as well as more faithful to ordinary understanding, to construe "aggression" broadly and insist on terms like "hostility" and "destructiveness" for situations in which aggression has turned into hatred or become so intense that violence is employed.

A number of other writers have encountered the same semantic problem. The neuropsychiatrist Paul Schilder writes:

It is difficult to distinguish between activity, which is a general characteristic of life, and aggressiveness. . . . This activity in aggressiveness has a close relation to motor drives and to instincts in general. It doubtless has its foundation in the organic structure, and its variations are in close relation to the child's constitution. Organic processes may influence the general output of energy. The hyperkinetic child shows a great increase, not only in activity, but also in aggressiveness.[10]

The psychoanalyst D. W. Winnicott is making the same point about human infants when he states, "At origin aggressiveness is almost synonymous with activity."[11] The American analyst Clara Thompson writes:

Aggression is not necessarily destructive at all. It springs from an innate tendency to grow and master life which seems to be characteristic of all living matter. Only when this life force is obstructed in its development do ingredients of anger, rage, or hate become connected with it.[12]

In another passage, Schilder says:

In his relation to plants and the inanimate world, man makes use of his strength. He has to destroy structures and use material without regard for their inner organization. A close relationship exists between such activities and aggressiveness towards animals and human beings. Thus, Freud has offered the theory that these "instincts of the ego," which serve self-preservation, are identical with the destructive tendencies, and that they are primarily directed toward one's self and only secondarily towards the outer world.[13]

The use of the term "instinct" by both Schilder and Freud is anachronistic, because it suggests that aggression is an innate drive requiring periodic discharge. As I pointed out earlier, no one now thinks of aggression in this way. However, if one makes allowance for his old-fashioned terminology, Freud's view that aggression and self-preservation are connected is in line with what I have argued thus far. Freud considered that aggression was derived from the so-called "death instinct" being redirected toward the external world. Very few analysts, with the exception of Melanie Klein, have accepted Freud's concept of a "death instinct," but since Freud is so centrally important in any consideration of human motivation, a brief explanation of what he meant is required.

Freud originally regarded aggression as a sadistic aspect of the sexual instinct, a primitive form of dominating or mastering the sexual object.

> Love in this form and at this preliminary stage [pregenital] is hardly to be distinguished from hate in its attitude toward the object. Not until the genital organization is established does love become the opposite of hate.
>
> Hate, as a relation to objects, is older than love. It derives from the narcissistic ego's primordial repudiation of the external world with its outpouring of stimuli. As an expression of the reaction of unpleasure evoked by objects, it always remains in intimate relation with the self-preservative instincts; so that sexual and ego-instincts can readily develop an antithesis which repeats that of love and hate. When the ego-instincts dominate the sexual function, as is the case at the stage of the

sadistic-anal organization, they impart the qualities of hate to the instinctual aim as well.[14]

The First World War may have influenced Freud in finally accepting the idea that aggression is independent of sex. His first full acknowledgment of this appears in his speculative paper *Beyond the Pleasure Principle*, which was not published until 1920. Freud observed that patients suffering from traumatic neuroses brought on by accidents or shock often had dreams in which the unpleasant event was repeated in undisguised form. He also noted that small children tended to repeat unpleasant experiences, such as the departure of a parent, by making them into a repetitive game. In both instances, repetition of intrinsically unpleasant events appeared to contravene the pleasure principle, that is, the idea that human behavior is primarily governed by the desire to obtain pleasure and to avoid pain.

Why would anyone want to recall and repeat an unpleasant experience? Freud thought that another principle must be at work. He concluded that both neurotics who had been exposed to trauma and children who had been exposed to distress were attempting to *master* their experiences by repeating them in dream and play. In fact, this tendency to repeat traumatic events in order to come to terms with them is not confined to dreams and childhood games. We must all have encountered friends who, after some loss or shock, feel compelled to tell the story of their misadventure at every opportunity until the incident eventually loses its emotional charge.

As the above quotation demonstrates, Freud thought that aggression and self-preservation were intimately connected. It must be remembered that Freud believed that the function of the mental apparatus was to rid the organism of disturbing stimuli, whether these impinged upon it from the external world or originated as instinctual tensions from within. In light of this belief, the fact that Freud linked aggression with the mastery of shock and distress by means of repetition becomes comprehensible. It is as if the sufferer were saying, "I will not allow this event to continue to cause me distress. I will diminish its emotional significance by repeatedly facing it. I will get on top of it; I won't allow it to get me down."

Our imagined subject is clearly *attacking* his problem in a positive fashion. His behavior also demonstrates the point that aggression need not be directed toward another person.

Freud came to believe that the compulsion to repeat was characteristic of all forms of behavior which he labeled "instinctive." Since the basic function of the mental apparatus was to get rid of stimuli and restore the organism to a former state of tranquility, Freud concluded, *"It seems, then, that an instinct is an urge inherent in organic life to restore an earlier stage of things* which the living entity has been obliged to abandon under the pressure of external disturbing forces."[15] Pursuing this idea to its logical conclusion, Freud then asked himself what was the earliest state of things which instinct was seeking to restore. Since the inorganic precedes the organic in the history of our planet, the ultimate aim must be to attain a state before life itself existed: "If we are to take it as a truth that knows no exception that everything living dies for *internal* reasons—becomes inorganic once again—then we shall be compelled to say that '*the aim of all life is death*' and, looking backwards, that '*inanimate things existed before living ones*.' "[16] This is Freud's exposition of what he called the "death instinct," the ultimate expression of the organism's striving to reach a condition of perfect peace where neither external nor internal stimuli can disturb it.

There are two main objections to such a theory. The first is that it does not make sense to regard all stimuli as disturbances the organism wants to be rid of. Both animals and men, when placed in environments where stimuli are minimal, such as zoos or solitary confinement, desperately search for stimuli and may even turn to self-injury in preference to nothing. The central nervous system requires input if it is to function effectively. The second objection is that it runs counter to biological common sense to suppose that there is an inbuilt drive to bring life to an end. It is true that every living creature dies; but this seems consequent upon wear and tear rather than any innate drive toward death.

However, Freud considered that aggression was derived from the redirection of the death instinct against the external world: "The instinct of destruction, moderated and tamed, and, as it were, inhibited in its aim, must, when it is directed toward objects, provide the ego with the satisfaction of its vital needs and with control over nature."[17]

We can accept Freud's idea that aggression is connected with the satisfaction of vital needs and with control over nature without following him in supposing that aggression is derived from a "death instinct." As I suggested above, aggression seems closely linked with self-preservation, self-assertion, and self-affirmation, and becomes converted into hatred and destructiveness only when self-preservation is threatened or self-affirmation is denied. If this way of considering the relation between aggression and destructiveness is valid, the sentence which opens D. W. Winnicott's important paper "Aggression in Relation to Emotional Development" seems less startling. "The main idea behind this study of aggression is that if society is in danger, it is not because of man's aggressiveness but because of the repression of personal aggressiveness in individuals."[18]

What Winnicott goes on to argue is that when personal aggressiveness is repressed, it turns into destructiveness and violence. If the individual's requirement to be recognized and appreciated as a person in his own right has not been met, the normal drive toward self-affirmation and self-assertion becomes intensified and transmuted into hostility. Aggression is liable to turn into dangerous violence when it is repressed or disowned. The man who is able to assert himself in a socially acceptable fashion is seldom vicious; it is the weak who are most likely to stab one in the back. As we shall see later, some types of multiple murderer appear to be so ordinary and so inoffensive that they make very little impression on those who meet them. It makes sense to suppose that such individuals, for whatever

21

reason, have been unsuccessful in achieving a sense of personal significance and identity, and that their violent acts represent the emergence of repressed aggression converted into destructive hatred. This is no more than a partial explanation of grossly abnormal human behavior, to which many other factors must also contribute.

Whilst repudiating the idea that men are furnished with an aggressive "instinct" demanding satisfaction in the same way as the sexual instinct, we must accept that the human species is endowed with a considerable potential for aggressive behavior which is biologically adaptive in origin, as in other species. All societies consist of individuals who both cooperate and compete with each other, who are simultaneously brothers and rivals. The degree to which mutual support or mutual competition predominates varies from society to society and from time to time. According to Michael Chance, studying the behavior of the higher primates makes it clear that we tend to function in one of two mental modes which he calls "agonic" and "hedonic."

> In one, *the agonic mode*, we are primarily concerned with self-security, and our attention is much taken up with being part of a group and with what others think of us so as to assure acceptance by the group. We become concerned with rank, hierarchy, convention, and maintaining good order, as an expression of this inbred security mechanism. In this mode our concerns are predominantly self-protective and engage information-processing systems that are specifically designed to attend, recognise, and respond to potential threats to our physical self, status, and social presentation.

In the other, *the hedonic mode*, we are more free to form a network of personal relationships that typically offer mutual support. Then we can also give free rein to our intelligence, our creativity, and the creation of systems of order in our thoughts and in our social relations. This is because attention, when released from self-protective needs, can be used to explore and integrate many new domains. Our mind may thus process information in two quite different ways.[19]

Throughout human history, men have imagined societies in which strife and rivalry have been abolished; in which, to use Chance's terminology, the agonic mode is entirely replaced by the hedonic mode. The Greek myth of the Isles of the Blessed and the Roman myth of a Golden Age both portray societies of this kind. The idea of an egalitarian community without competition is a revolutionary myth with a powerful appeal to the oppressed. Competition between individuals can certainly be reduced or encouraged, as differing educational and political experiments have shown; but it can never be abolished, because it is based upon a deeply rooted "aggressive" component of human nature which is needed for self-preservation and self-affirmation. Even when men and women share belief systems and ideals, and form associations of like-minded people on this basis, it is never long before differences emerge.

It is curious and deplorable that beliefs, whether political, religious, or psychoanalytic, become so emotionally important that they turn people into fanatics. It is a reflection of our basic insecurity that any accepted faith purporting to explain our relation with the universe often becomes so integral to our identity that we treat attacks upon our faith as attacks upon ourselves. For example, differences of opinion between psychoanalysts have often been passionate and bitter. The history of the psychoanalytic movement is disfigured by dissension, sometimes leading to the formation of rival groups by rebels against Freud's dogmatism. Adler, Stekel, Jung, Rank, and many others were abused and vilified by the orthodox. At a later period, the British Psycho-Analytical Society was nearly split in two by disputes between analysts grouped around Melanie Klein and those who could not accept her findings. It is perhaps only to be expected that the psychoanalyst who, more than any other, attributed intense feelings of rage and destructiveness to the infant in arms should herself be the center of violent controversy.

Animals are bound to compete with each other unless the environment is so abundant that there is more than enough for all. Since competition for resources is inevitable, individuals cannot remain viable without some method of ensuring that competing animals do not destroy each other. Nor is it only aggressive competition between individuals which constitutes a threat. In the absence of checks and balances, the environment is habitually overexploited, with the result that the terrain dries up as a source of sustenance.

In animals other than man, the preservation of individuals is secured by conventions which prevent aggressive competition from turning into destructive hostility. One such convention, extensively studied amongst birds, is territorial behavior. The adoption of a

24

piece of territory from which competitors are excluded results in a defensible food supply and the dispersion of nests. Birdsong has a number of different functions, which include providing evidence of the singer's location and readiness to mate. But one of the commonest and most important varieties of song is territorial: a warning to intruders to keep off the patch of land the singer is defending. In some species, prolonged skirmishes occur along territorial boundaries; but these seldom result in actual contact between rivals.

Man has extended competition for resources to many other things besides food, from gold to oil wells. Even in societies which provide a high level of material comfort, people compete with each other. Man's capacity for symbolization ensures that money and material possessions have a psychological significance which transcends their intrinsic nature and makes them into objects which enhance status and that personal sense of significance we all seek. Because he tends to defend his native land and his home with especial vigor, man is often labeled territorial. Regrettably, vocal warnings and conventional skirmishes are not enough to deter rival groups of men from crossing territorial boundaries, seizing what they want, and killing or capturing those who stand in their way.

Another convention is the substitution of threat and display for actual combat; or, in cases where fighting occurs, the adoption of gestures of defeat or submission which have the effect of making the winner desist from further attack. Anyone who has watched television films of animal behavior knows that contests between male rivals for available females take place during the breeding season. This is generally thought to be adaptive, since such contests ensure that the strongest or most attractive males have the best chance of reproducing themselves. Although quite severe injuries may occasionally be inflicted, defeated rivals are not usually pursued or killed, and most survive to fight another day. It used to be thought that animals of the same species practically never killed each other unless there was an intense struggle for survival occasioned by severe shortage of food. In fact, prolonged observation has shown that intraspecific killing exists in many species. Creatures which form clans or colonies may destroy members of any other colony which stray into their midst. This behavior has been observed in social insects, such as bees, termites, and ants, and in rats and other rodents. The attack may be triggered by the different smell of the intruder. Pitched battles have also been observed between rival groups of hyenas competing for a kill. On rare occasions, male chimpanzees have been observed invading the territories of other groups and killing their male members. Conventions and rituals do not always prevent serious conflict.

Lingering remnants of ritualization can be detected in some forms of human conflict. "Hitting a man when he is down" is still deplored in sporting circles. Disputes between rivals in Eskimo societies are sometimes settled by song contests. Some research workers have claimed that conflicts between rival groups of soccer fans are more in the nature of "macho" displays than dangerous fights. Recent tragedies at soccer matches throw doubt upon this finding; but all kinds of other factors affect such situations, including the availability of alcohol, the design of stadiums, and the effectiveness of methods of crowd control. Young men, especially, seem to need opportunities for aggressive display and rivalry which Western civilization does not easily provide; and it may be the case that such contests would be highly ritualized if we created the right conditions. In at least some of the hunter-gatherer societies in which war between neighboring tribes is endemic and almost continuous, very few people get killed. Peter Matthiessen, describing a war between rival groups in New Guinea, writes:

> The shouted war was increasing in ferocity, and several men from each side would dance out and feign attacks, whirling and prancing to display their splendour. They were jeered and admired by both sides and were not shot at, for display and panoply were part of war, which was less war than ceremonial sport, a wild, fierce festival. . . . A day of war was dangerous and splendid, regardless of its outcome; it was a war of individuals and gallantry, quite innocent of tactics and cold slaughter. A single death on either side would mean victory or defeat.[20]

But the invention of weapons which kill at long distances has overridden the conventions which might still be partially operative if human battles were confined to fisticuffs or had not progressed beyond the employment of spears and arrows.

In recent years, there has been a good deal of argument about how animal populations regulate their

27

numbers. Rapid increase can take place under some circumstances, especially when a species is put into a new environment where no balance with predators or competitor species exists. This was what happened when rabbits were introduced into Australia, where they became a serious pest. When six pheasants were placed on an island, their population increased to 1,898 individuals in only six years.[21] In the first edition of this book, I referred to the theories advanced by V. C. Wynne-Edwards, who thought that communities of birds developed systems of communication signaling population density. When the population became excessive, he supposed that a number of individuals reduced the breeding capacity of the community by refusing to mate or by removing themselves. Today most authorities think that natural selection acts upon the individual rather than the group, and that shortage of food is the principal reason populations tend to remain fairly stable rather than increasing immoderately. When populations are high, a larger proportion die. When populations are low and food resources relatively plentiful, more individuals survive.

Industrialization has made man biologically inept. The environment has been so ruthlessly exploited in many parts of the world that nations are at last meeting to try and prevent further destruction of the rain forests and the ozone layer, and to call a halt to industrial pollution of the air, the rivers, and the oceans. Whether they can succeed before irrevocable changes take place in the earth's climate remains uncertain.

Modern agriculture and medicine have ensured that far more members of the human race than ever before survive the hazards of birth and infancy and live on into old age. Although the invention of efficient methods of contraception may have reduced the birth rate in selected groups, human population as a whole continues to grow at an alarming pace. Wherever hygiene is taught, diet improved, and medical facilities introduced, infant mortality declines and the birth rate increases. Famine and disease are still endemic in many parts of the world; but such primitive checks on population growth are repugnant to humanitarian feelings. We cannot withhold the benefits of modern techniques of agriculture and preventive medicine from those who urgently need them. But we must insist that family limitation go hand in hand with the provision of such technologies.

Overcrowding is one cause of stress which tends to convert competitive aggression into violence in some animal societies. Calhoun's experiments with rats showed that overcrowding not only caused violence but many other behavioral disturbances, including cannibalism.[22] Increased violence has been observed amongst captive troops of monkeys when the size of their enclosure was suddenly reduced. Solly Zuckerman's famous study of the baboons on Monkey Hill in the London Zoo should have been entitled *The Abnormal Social Life of Baboons under Stress of Confinement* rather than *The Social Life of Monkeys and Apes*.[23] As long ago as 1969, Adolph Schultz wrote:

The relation between different groups of a population of wild primates will rarely degenerate into actual fighting, being mostly settled by means of long-range threatening or mere warning signals, if not by the discreet withdrawal of the smaller party. . . . From the many recent field studies it has become evident that nonhuman primates under natural conditions and regardless of differences in their social systems, generally lead peaceful lives and are certainly not nearly as aggressive and easily provoked creatures as used to be assumed from their behaviour under crowded conditions of captivity.[24]

In human societies, it is difficult to be sure to what extent overcrowding itself contributes to such phenomena as violent crime, for overcrowding marches in lockstep with poverty, ill health, and all the other undesirable features of inner city life. Moreover, tolerance of proximity varies from culture to culture. American and Japanese ideas of what constitutes crowding are very different. Individuals also vary. Some studies suggest that men who are repeatedly violent without obvious provocation are hypersensitive to the approach of others and tend to interpret proximity as threatening. Fear of attack and the unjustified imputation of hostile intent to others are potent instigators of violence both between individuals and between nations. Although nuclear weapons have made the possibility of war so terrible as to deter those powers which possess such weapons from using them, the threat of global destruction still exists, and men still destroy each other in conventional warfare.

It is clear that human beings possess a marked

hereditary predisposition toward aggressive behavior which they share with other animals and which serves a number of positive functions. An animal has to be able to compete for whatever resources of food are available. Sexual selection is ensured by competition for mates. Territorial animals have to be able to defend their territories. Animals which live in groups tend to establish hierarchies which reduce conflict between individuals; and wide-ranging groups respond to dominant males who act as leaders at times of threat from predators. All these biologically adaptive aspects of aggression can be found in man. We are bound to recognize that man's predisposition toward aggression is partially innate; and we must also acknowledge its positive functions. We have to be able to defend ourselves against enemies, to give orders or to obey in circumstances of danger, and to compete with our fellows when necessary for reproduction or survival. Because human beings are complex, and especially because we have the capacity for symbolization, our aggressive potential manifests itself in a variety of metaphorical ways which, as demonstrated above, have become enshrined in "aggressive" language. We need to be able to attack difficulties, to defeat problems, to stand up for ourselves, to define our separate identities, and to affirm ourselves as individuals, if we are to achieve a sense of personal significance and competence.

In this connection, the study of depressive illness is illuminating. Those suffering from severe depression feel both helpless and hopeless; and we regularly find that such feelings are the consequence of repressing

31

aggression. Depressed patients have thrown out the baby with the bath water. By repressing violent feelings which they dare not express or even recognize, they have deprived themselves of those positive aspects of aggression which subserve an individual's sense of his own value and make it possible for him to tackle problems with confidence.

What we need to explore and understand is how and why aggression becomes transmuted into destructive violence. Why are human beings not content to let defeated enemies go, instead of often vindictively pursuing them even when immediate objectives have been attained? Why do people engage in deliberate cruelty? Are violent and destructive individuals invariably pathological? How easy is it to turn a normal man into a torturer? What motivates those who inflict savage injuries on the helpless? Is violence chiefly motivated by anger or by fear?

Some of these questions are explored in the pages which follow. No one knows all the answers to these problems; but since psychiatrists see a variety of individuals who either behave destructively or else complain of difficulty in controlling impulses toward violence and cruelty, the contribution of psychiatry is not irrelevant. Certain kinds of upbringing predispose children to believe that desires and emotions which can be found in everybody are peculiar to themselves. Some patients consult psychiatrists because they are horrified to discover aggressive impulses within themselves which are in fact normal. Others have so repressed their hostility that they have also inhibited their drive toward independence and their capacity for initiative. Such people live in a permanent state of depression. Others display irritability and hostility in response to minimal stimuli most people would ignore. The study of unusual individuals can throw light upon "normal" aggression in exactly the same way that the study of disease in a bodily organ can help us to understand that organ's normal function.

In any society, there are unusually violent individuals who used to be labeled "aggressive psychopaths" or "sociopaths." Today they are generally said to be manifesting a sociopathic or asocial personality disorder. There are also sadists, although the term "sadism" is widely misused to describe any kind of cruel behavior. I shall argue that the study of man's paranoid potential reveals more about human cruelty and destructiveness than the study of aggressive personality disorders or sadomasochism; but discussion of both these topics is a necessary preliminary.

# 2

---

## *Aggressive Personality Disorders*

BOTH THE World Health Organization and the American Psychiatric Association have recognized the need for some diagnostic classification which can be applied to individuals who used to be called "aggressive psychopaths." ICD9 (the Ninth Revision of the International Classification of Diseases) offers "personality disorder with predominantly sociopathic or asocial manifestation." The draft Tenth Revision is considering substituting the word "dyssocial" for "asocial." DSM-III-R (the third edition of the *Diagnostic and Statistical Manual of*

*Mental Disorders*) refers to "antisocial personality disorder." These classifications have largely, though not completely, displaced the term "psychopath," which, as I pointed out in the first edition of this book, has been used to describe such a wide variety of unusual human beings that it has become almost meaningless except as a label indicating disapproval or lack of comprehension. However, the British Mental Health Act of 1983 still refers to "psychopathic disorder," which it defines as "a persistent disorder or disability of mind (whether or not including significant impairment of intelligence) which results in abnormally aggressive or seriously irresponsible conduct on the part of the person concerned."

Although the various authorities who deal with classification may disagree about terminology, they all recognize the existence in Western societies of a minority of individuals responsible for a high proportion of violent crime. These individuals, from an early age, are unusually egotistical, callous, and impulsive. They feel no obligation to be truthful and lie without hesitation where their own interests are involved. Some become habitual liars who make up fantastic tales designed to convince others (and themselves) of their own importance. They tend to grab what they want, irrespective of the claims or rights of other people, and do not hesitate to use violence if obstructed. They usually exhibit little capacity for foresight, are undeterred by the threat of punishment, and are unresponsive to punishment of any kind when it is inflicted. Indeed, punishment often exacerbates their latent hostility to their fellows. Their lack of foresight is connected with a general failure to control the impulse of the moment. This may account for the fact that there is considerable overlap between those who commit crimes of violence and those who commit sexual crimes or dangerous driving offenses.

The existence of such people as a definable group of abnormals has been recognized since the beginning of the nineteenth century. But there are still disagreement and doubt about the nature of their abnormality and its possible causes. Is it genetic in origin or associated with intellectual defect? Is lack of control and foresight a disturbance of cerebral function, comparable with the temporary impairments exhibited by those under the influence of alcohol or other drugs, or with the permanent defects found in those affected by brain disease or injury? Or do these people behave in antisocial ways because their childhood environment was one of deprivation and punishment? If such a childhood environment predisposes the individual to violence and cruelty, is his behavior revenge for real or imagined neglect and rejection? Or is it that such an environment both discourages social integration and encourages the habitual employment of violence? Should such people be considered mentally ill? And whether they are labeled mentally ill or not, should they be treated as responsible for their antisocial behavior?

Some of these questions can be given definite answers; others await the findings of further research. A few are dependent on assumptions and modes of thinking which, I shall argue, are out of date and should be discarded.

One possibility, now disproved, is that aggressive

personality disorder is genetically determined by abnormalities of the sex chromosomes. Although males who possess an extra sex chromosome (XXY and XYY) have a somewhat increased risk for admission to mental hospitals, the idea that they are unusually aggressive has been shown to be a myth. The great majority do not get into trouble with the law.[1]

This finding does not imply that genetic factors play no part in antisocial behavior. Eysenck suggests that the majority of delinquents and criminals are highly extraverted by nature. Extraverts are more resistant to conditioning than introverts, and are therefore less likely to accept and incorporate normal social restraints upon aggressive behavior. Eysenck believes that criminality is largely determined by inheritance.[2] This supposition finds some support from other sources.

> The idea of the born criminal, or at least the inheritance of a predisposition to crime, was once extremely popular. Now, with our democratic desire to believe that everybody starts equal, we have swung towards the other extreme, attributing the lion's share of responsibility to family and social environment. But the stubborn fact remains that, from the beginning, individuals react differently to very similar circumstances. A study of Danish children adopted at birth demonstrated that their criminal records were more likely to resemble those of their natural fathers than those of their adopters, quite striking evidence that some genetic factor was at work and that environment and upbringing are not all-powerful.[3]

Although people classified as mentally handicapped or subnormal are overrepresented amongst petty recidivist criminals, lack of intelligence is not a major factor in aggressive behavior. Most mentally handicapped people lack the initiative to engage in major crime, and provided they receive sufficient support from family or friends, they lead uneventful, placid lives which constitute no threat to others.

It is widely recognized that some people become aggressive after drinking alcohol. But the extent to which excessive consumption of alcohol is involved in a variety of crimes is still insufficiently appreciated. Forty to fifty percent of those incarcerated in penal institutions in the United States have had serious drinking problems. One study of homicides in the Philadelphia area concluded that in nearly two-thirds of the cases, the offender or the victim or both had been drinking immediately before the killing.[4] Every lawyer and criminologist will be familiar with cases in which a quarrel breaks out in a bar between two men who have been drinking together, to be followed by a fight in which one man kills the other. The killer is sometimes immediately overcome with remorse, and may protest that he has mistakenly killed a friend or relative with whom he usually had a warm relationship. If governments had the courage to triple the price of alcohol, there is no doubt that the incidence of violent crime would be greatly reduced.

Alcohol is not the only substance which breaks down the controls that normally inhibit violence. Amphetamines, barbiturates, and other drugs may have the same effect. Narcotics like heroin and morphine inhibit initiative and reduce activity whilst the user is under their influence. But addiction to such drugs creates so intense a craving for them that addicts often commit violent robbery to get the money they require for new supplies. This type of crime dominates some urban areas and is often associated with gang warfare and homicide.

Diabetics whose insulin requires regulation may suffer episodes of hypoglycemia, that is, of lowered blood sugar. This condition also occurs when someone produces too much insulin because he is suffering from a tumor of the insulin-producing cells, an insulinoma. For example:

> A 27-year-old man was referred as a psychiatric emergency on account of bouts of aggressive and destructive behaviour. He showed disorientation and inappropriate behaviour during attacks, with sweating and violent tremor, and had no subsequent recollection of what had occurred. . . . Prolonged fasting provoked a typical attack at 16 hours, associated with hypoglycaemia and relieved by glucose.[5]

This man was subsequently found to have multiple tumors of the insulin-producing cells of the pancreas.

Hypoglycemia, alcohol, and certain other drugs, including amphetamines, have in common the effect of reducing the amount of serotonin in the brain. It appears that serotonin, a neurotransmitter, is an important component of the neural mechanism inhibiting aggression. Certain diets may have similar effects.

Periods of famine and general protein and carbohydrate malnutrition have historically been associated with great increases in criminality and violence, and it has recently been reported that countries above the median in corn consumption have significantly higher homicide rates than those whose corn consumption is below the median. Corn consumption has been seen experimentally to result in low levels of brain serotonin.[6]

Epilepsy has long been associated with outbursts of aggressive behavior, especially when the focus of the epileptic discharge is found to be in the temporal lobes. Some patients suffering from temporal lobe epilepsy have been treated by surgical removal of the affected area. In general, brain operations designed to control aggression have had such variable results that they are now seldom employed. Ethical considerations forbid the use of brain surgery in the treatment of violent offenders and juveniles who are not capable of giving unbiased, informed consent to such irreversible procedures.

Further evidence linking disturbance of brain function with aggression is found in studying the electroencephalogram (EEG). Personality disorders involving antisocial conduct are especially likely to be associated with abnormal electrical activity in the temporal lobes. In such cases, the EEG abnormalities reflect cerebral immaturity, in that the brain waves are of a type generally found in children rather than adults. The supposition that some cases of aggressive personality disorder are related to delay in the process of maturation is supported by the fact that aggressive and antisocial behavior declines with age.

> A more recent study by Williams (1969) has reinforced the importance of earlier findings. In a review of EEG's carried out on 333 men convicted of violent crimes he divided the population into two groups—206 who had a history of habitual aggression or explosive rage, and 127 who had committed an isolated act of aggression. In the first group the aggression appeared to be largely endogenous and personality related, and in the second to be provoked by unusually stressful environmental factors. Sixty-five per cent of the habitually aggressive offenders had abnormal EEG's compared to only 24 per cent of the remainder. Eighty per cent of both groups showed dysrhythmias known to be associated with temporal lobe dysfunction.[7]

However, EEGs are notoriously difficult to evaluate. A review of one hundred children with severe psychiatric disorders failed to demonstrate any association between EEG abnormalities localized in the temporal lobe and aggressive or antisocial behavior.[8] Further long-term studies of how EEGs change over time in disturbed individuals are required.

Head injury, various viral diseases affecting the brain, and some cerebral tumors may also be responsible for uncontrolled aggressive behavior. These observations strongly suggest that many people who exhibit the characteristic features of aggressive personality disorder are suffering from impairment of the control systems of the brain consequent upon persistent immaturity, brain damage, or toxic impairment of brain function.

However, it is true that many of those classified as suffering from aggressive personality disorder do not have abnormal EEGs or any form of brain disease or other physical abnormality. It is also the case that many people who have abnormal EEGs are not particularly aggressive. In other words, although there may be constitutional factors which predispose an individual to violence, these factors alone do not guarantee that violence will manifest itself.

How far does the early environment of individuals with aggressive personality disorder account for their behavior? Most authorities agree that family background is an important determinant of future antisocial and violent behavior. A variety of studies concur in concluding that aggressive youths frequently come from families in which the parents are cold, rejecting, physically punitive, and at odds with each other. In 1972 I quoted Leonard Berkowitz on this point, and subsequent research has confirmed what he wrote in his book *Aggression*, first published in 1962.

> There is a remarkable consistency to these findings. The studies reviewed here agree in noting that *punitive parental disciplinary methods* (such as physical punishment and depriving children of privileges) *tend to be associated with a high level of aggression and other forms of antisocial behavior by the children. Love-oriented disciplinary methods*, on the other hand, *evidently facilitate the development of conscience and internalized restraints against socially disap-*

43

*proved behavior*. Praising the child when he complies with parental standards and reasoning with him when he does not apparently are among the most effective of these love-oriented techniques.[9]

Whilst confirming the association between exposure to physical punishment and later aggressiveness, however, some researchers have questioned whether it is a direct expression of cause and effect.

It may be that this association reflects the tendency of children to imitate the aggressive behaviour of their parents, or it may be that aggressive children tend to elicit harsh treatment from their parents. Another possibility is that there is no causal link between harsh parental punishment and aggressive children, and that the two only appear to be related because of the operation of a third factor. For example, it may be that harsh parental punishment and aggressive children are both more common in low income families, and that this explains the association.[10]

I quote this to demonstrate how difficult it is to assess all the various factors which may combine to cause antisocial and aggressive behavior. My own view is that Berkowitz is right. The development of conscience as an internal regulator of behavior depends more upon the wish to preserve the love and esteem of those close to one than it does upon the fear of punishment. That is, a child who has been loved by his parents will gradually make their moral standards his own and learn to conform to what they expect, because he wishes to keep his parents' love and fears its withdrawal. In families where mutual love prevails, the child's self-esteem becomes dependent upon continuity of love. Punishment, especially physical punishment, has the effect of increasing resentment and hostility; and although severe punishment may cause a child to suppress overt hostility for fear of reprisal, it is not so effective a creator of conscience as fear of the withdrawal of love.

If a child does not receive love from parents during its early years, it will not incorporate their standards and develop a normal conscience. Moreover, parents who show little love are often inconsistent and unpredictable and may not establish any reliable standards of behavior within the family. In addition to a lack of restraint over the aggressive impulses common to all children, the loveless child tends to experience an intensification of these impulses. It seems that human beings, as social animals, have a basic need for acceptance and approval. They react to love's absence with resentment, even though they may not appear to know what they are missing. Children who have not developed conscience as an internal regulator of behavior may restrain their aggression only if there is a clear threat of immediate punishment. Children who have developed a normal conscience tend to behave well even when there is no immediate threat of punishment.

It is obvious that if withdrawal of love is to operate as an effective sanction, there must be some love between parent and child in the first place. A child cannot respond to the withdrawal of something he has never had. It can be argued that every baby must have had some experience of being cuddled, caressed, and cared for; babies without any such experience are unlikely to survive. But many children receive so little affection that their self-esteem comes to depend upon their toughness rather than their lovableness; and it is not surprising to discover that a high proportion of the pathologically aggressive are the products of broken homes, loveless homes, or impersonal institutions. Lack of affection and discord between parents increase the likelihood of future delinquency in children.

There is growing evidence that many of the adverse effects of early deprivation and ill-treatment can be considerably modified by later favorable experiences. It follows that even when children have been severely damaged by their early environment, remedial measures like adoption may still produce valuable changes. Yet it remains the case that many of the most deprived spend their entire childhood in the unfavorable environment in which they began life and therefore have little chance of learning to improve their social relationships.[11]

It is clear that the same lack of close positive relationships which precludes the development of a normal conscience accounts for the failure of antisocial personalities to identify with other human beings or care what they suffer. We expect that a small child will regard even those who look after him from a "selfish" angle. The younger the child, the more will he think of other people as instruments to provide for his own needs, and the less will he consider them as having needs of their own.

The appreciation of other people as beings entitled to as much consideration as himself comes later in childhood and develops only on the basis of positive bonds of attachment. Those who have experienced love in childhood gradually learn to care for others reciprocally and to appreciate that the people who look after them have a need for love in return. As they develop, they learn not to hurt other people's feelings and to give as well as take. At the lowest level, they find that consideration for others pays, since it leads to obtaining more love and hence more self-esteem.

Where love is absent, or where some innate physical or psychological defect makes the individual incapable of responding to love, the conditions for learning to appreciate the needs and separate existence of others are simply not present. It is therefore understandable that antisocial personalities disregard the rights of other people, value them only insofar as they satisfy immediate needs, and do not feel guilt at inflicting pain and suffering on those who obstruct them.

This is not quite so far from normal as might at first appear. Even the best-balanced, most loving human being is capable of only a limited range of sympathies. It is difficult for most of us to care deeply about those who are not within our own circles of relatives and friends. We may be shocked by famine in Africa, by earthquakes in Turkey, or by tidal waves in Japan; but these disasters do not touch our hearts in the same way as do our own bereavements or those of our friends. Antisocial personalities tend to regard even those in their immediate environment with the same indifference an American

47

might display toward an unknown peasant in China. Because other people mean so little to them, it is not surprising that these abnormal individuals show scant remorse for violence or other infringements of human rights.

The absence of interpersonal bonds also explains the characteristic disregard for truth in the antisocial. If other people are simply "fair game," there is no more reason to be honest with them than there is to tell the truth to the enemy in wartime. The behavior of many antisocial individuals suggests that they live in a world they assume to be either actively hostile or else indifferent to their welfare. If lying is more likely to gain what they want than telling the truth, they will lie with no more guilt than a captured soldier feels when he lies to his captors. Particularly interesting are the pathological liars known in Britain as "false pretenders," confidence tricksters who make up fantastic stories about themselves to obtain money and other advantages. There is some overlap between this type of antisocial individual and those who habitually employ violence. One example is the British murderer Neville Heath, who, in addition to killing two women, posed as a high-ranking army officer and as an English aristocrat. Although habitual lying can be regarded as aggressive behavior, many false pretenders are not violent; but to pursue their psychology further would take us too far from our main theme.

In the first chapter, I drew attention to the difference between "hostile" aggression and "instrumental" aggression. A good deal of criminal violence is clearly instrumental, that is, casual rather than deliberate. The robber who clubs his victim may not care what the latter feels, but he is not deliberately exercising cruelty. Criminologists have experimented with bringing violent offenders face to face with those they have assaulted. In some instances, these confrontations have brought home to the offender for the first time the realization that his victim is a human being like himself, with the consequence that he has wished to make reparation.

Other violent offenders are much more difficult to handle because they are full of hatred rather than simply indifferent. By way of illustration, it is worth quoting from one of Tony Parker's interviews with an inmate in the British prison Grendon Underwood. The subject is an Irishman of thirty, an alcoholic with convictions for "grievous bodily harm." An illegitimate child, with no idea of who his father was, he was brought up by a series of his mother's relatives.

> I can't explain it properly: you know you've been robbed of something and as soon as you were born you were an embarrassment and a nuisance. I wasn't wanted right from the start, that's plain enough for sure, and I think it makes you grow up on the defensive and hating other people all the time because you know you're not a fully fledged member of their society. So you turn your back on it, you don't even want to behave as though you are. You think, "Oh sod the lot of you then, I don't care for you no more than you care for me.". . .
> 　　—I hate this place, I hate the screws, I hate eating the food they give me and wearing the clothes they tell

me I have to put on. I hate everybody, that's the fact of it; and most of all I hate myself. Hatred, violence, I'm full of it. I think if I had the chance I'd destroy the whole world.[12]

It is understandable that such an individual is not deterred by punishment, which he merely regards as further evidence of society's rejection. Certainly he is incapable of being affected by society's disapproval, since he never experienced any approval in the first place.

The threat of punishment deters normal people far more effectively than it does the habitually violent, because normal people care about the disapproval of society as well as the penalty inflicted. That the former is a more important deterrent than the latter is shown by the history of the penal code, which demonstrates that there is little correlation between severity of punishment and deterrent effect. In 1814, Sir Samuel Romilly attempted to persuade the British Parliament that the penalty of hanging, drawing, and quartering could safely be abolished. He failed to do so, for many members of Parliament claimed that there would be an immediate increase in the crimes of treason for which this barbarous method of execution was still the prescribed penalty. Similar fears were expressed when it was first proposed to abolish hanging as a punishment for theft. Yet the evidence suggests that the ordinary person will be deterred from crime by comparatively minor penalties when these are combined with a high expectation that the crime will be detected, whilst antisocial personalities will not be deterred by even the most savage penalties and will probably behave worse after such penalties have been inflicted. It is natural enough that we should wish to revenge ourselves upon criminals who rape old ladies or torture children; but paradoxically, the people whom we most wish to punish are those least likely to respond to punishment. Another example from one of Tony Parker's studies of criminals dates from a time before flogging had been abolished in Britain.

> I should think the product I am today ought to prove thrashings are no good, and only produce responses of vengeance and violence. It makes me laugh when I read of the Tory women at Bournemouth calling for a return of the cat. Even on what you might call simply an economic basis, I and all the people I know would prefer the cat to a long sentence any time. After three days it doesn't hurt any more, and the scars soon heal except those on your mind. What you feel is anger, resentment, and, most of all, a determination somehow to get your own back. But being deterred? The idea never gets a look in.[13]

As an extreme example of childhood rejection and ill-treatment as a cause of violent behavior, I will cite the case of "Tom" from Muriel Gardiner's study of child murderers.[14] Tom was the third of eleven children. He was brought up by a mother who hated him. He was forbidden to mix with the rest of the family, forced to sleep in an unheated shed by himself, and given only one inadequate meal a day. Even when the law insisted that he go to school, he was not allowed to walk with his brothers and sisters and was whipped if he tried to mix with them. Tom suffered from rickets, eczema, and asthma. Eventually he became a delinquent, stole food, and was brought before the local court. A probation officer discovered the home situation, and Tom was sent to live with an aunt who unfortunately died within a year. Tom landed with another aunt whose husband was a violent heavy drinker. He found a little cat with a broken leg which he took home and tenderly cared for. The cat seems to have been the first living creature with which Tom formed ties of deep affection. One afternoon, Tom's uncle returned early from work after drinking heavily and found Tom playing with the cat. In a fit of rage, he strangled the cat in front of Tom and later stamped on the cross over the grave Tom had dug. At this point Tom went into the furnace room, picked up one of his uncle's loaded guns, and shot his uncle, his aunt, and his uncle's sister. He was fourteen years old and was sentenced to life imprisonment.

This case illustrates a number of factors linking ill-treatment in childhood with later violence. Isolation prevented Tom from forming bonds of attachment with either parents or siblings, which not only deprived him of love but also of any opportunity to learn how to handle aggression. Repeated abuse and humiliation induced a sense of chronic resentment. The ultimate provocation he received was extreme, but his response of triple murder can be understood only if one takes into account the whole history of his childhood. Tom had been made a scapegoat by his mother. Who can doubt that his final act of murder not only was an immediate response to his uncle's cruelty but also contained elements of revenge for his childhood rejection and humiliation? Human beings have long memories; and violent acts which seem disproportionately savage compared with the triggering incident are often avenging the past as well as reacting to the present.

Most of this chapter has been concerned with the uncontrolled and habitually violent, but Tom's triple murder was an isolated act committed by an adolescent who had not shown any previous tendency toward violence and who was in fact inept at defending or asserting himself. It has long been recognized that in addition to the antisocial personalities already discussed, there is another group of persons who commit extreme acts of violence and are usually overcontrolled rather than undercontrolled. It is postulated that people who are inhibited about the expression of anger and resentment build up hostile tension to the point where some provocation suddenly precipitates an explosively violent act, as in Tom's case. I suggested above that memories of past ill-treatment must have contributed to the violence of Tom's crime; but it must be admitted that this is an unfashionable view, because it presents hostile tension on a "hydraulic model," that is, as something which can build up inside an individual over a long period until it is finally discharged in a cathartic torrent. Modern research tends to dispute the validity of this model, affirming that states of frustration and resentment persist only when constantly reinforced by external stimulation. However, such research does not account for the well-known phenomenon of the man who abreacts the accumulated irritation of a bad day at the office by kicking the dog or shouting at his children. If resentment can be stored for hours, why not for days, for weeks, or even for a lifetime?

Although I reject the hydraulic model of aggression as an instinct needing periodic discharge, I find it difficult to believe that undischarged resentment is not stored in the long-term memory. Traumatic experiences have long-term effects, whether or not they occur in childhood. For example, studies of those confined in concentration camps demonstrate that after release survivors showed a "chronic stress syndrome" from which most never recovered. Amongst many other psychological symptoms, irritability was prominent. It is surely likely that this irritability was, at any rate in part, a manifestation of chronic resentment at mistreatment by their captors.

Victims of violent crime do not rapidly recover from the experience. After initial periods of shock and denial followed by fright and fear of recurrence, a third phase ensues in which apathy and anger may alternate.

The period of apathy after the crime may be prolonged and accompanied by feelings of anger toward society in general: "there is no justice," "no-one gives a damn." Anger is usually absent during the offence, presumably because the victim senses that expression of anger may threaten his life. Afterwards anger may be directed inwardly with resulting depression, guilt and self-blame. Directed outwardly the targets may be direct (the offender) or indirect. In the latter case the police, the justiciary, doctors or newspaper reporters may be accused of treating the victim poorly. When directed against the offender the victim may be accused of being preoccupied with revenge: the victim may feel or voice uncharacteristic violent or even murderous thoughts, sometimes progressing to intents or even to carrying them out.[15]

These examples suggest that anger unexpressed at the time of the traumata which provoke it is indeed "stored up" or repressed, only to emerge later, perhaps inappropriately. Anger is not the only emotion to be repressed in this way. Every psychiatrist has seen examples of incomplete mourning, of patients who have suffered severe bereavement but for a variety of reasons were unable to come to terms with their loss at the time of its occurrence. In psychotherapy, such patients may discover to their surprise that they are still mourning a loss they had supposed long since surmounted, and may find themselves shedding tears they could not allow to flow freely before.

There may be other explanations for the worm suddenly turning, as Kevin Howells suggests:

> Behaviourists might emphasize, for example, that the "meek," overcontrolled person may be prone to occasional extreme violence because he is incapable of acting sufficiently assertively to stop the provocation from another person. Persons unskilled in behaviour which might enable them not to be "picked on" are likely to be constantly re-exposed to a high, perhaps escalating level

of provocation. Intervening cognitive processes might also explain the sudden change from overcontrolled to explosively violent behaviour. The overcontrolled person may, over a period of time, change his constructions and interpretations of events, other people, relationships and of himself to such an extent that anger or other violence-generating affects increase and precipitate an incident.[16]

Whatever the mechanism involved, it was true until recently that extreme violence of homicidal intensity was more likely to be perpetrated by a usually controlled or overcontrolled member of the victim's family than by a stranger. I add the caveat "until recently" because in certain cities drug-related violence is now so prevalent that street murders exceed domestic murders. Before drug-related violence became common, less than twenty percent of adult male and female victims were killed by strangers. Murder was most often a crime in which men killed their wives, their mistresses, or their children, or in which women killed their children. Moreover, disputes leading to serious violence were often initiated by the victim, who was the first to use physical force in about one-third of the cases. "In summary," writes Howells, "serious violence often occurs between people who are intimately related and appears to occur following angry disputes and altercations."[17]

Domestic murderers, therefore, seldom belong to the group of persons classified as exhibiting "antisocial personality disorder." Although such murderers tend to be regarded with horror and are still subjected to severe penalties, many of them seem to be ordinary people who have been intolerably provoked. Most of us know what it is to experience feelings of rage, and we can imagine that we might express that rage in physically violent ways if we had been drinking or were sufficiently taunted. We recognize that it is those who know us best, our nearest and dearest, who have the power to humiliate and arouse us. Domestic murderers are comprehensible. It is far more difficult for the average citizen to identify with the habitually violent, or even with recidivist criminals who are not violent. They are perceived as belonging to a different subculture from that of the more or less law-abiding average citizen, whereas domestic murderers are people like us. Because murder is so often a "one-off" crime which is unlikely to be repeated, it is certain that we are confining for unnecessarily long periods many murderers who might safely be paroled. Society needs protection from antisocial personalities more than it does from domestic murderers.

In our present state of knowledge, it is not possible to pinpoint one predominant cause of antisocial personality disorders. As with most types of psychiatric disorder, the causes are multiple. Genetic factors, disturbances of brain function, broken homes, and cruel or neglectful parents are all important determinants of future aggressive behavior. So is being reared in a milieu where violence is habitually employed as punishment or as a way of settling disputes. But none of these factors inevitably produces a person who is habitually aggressive. Some human beings continue to be peaceable, well-behaved citizens in spite of genetic disadvantage and grossly adverse social conditions. Others who started life with many advantages may turn into habitual criminals. We are unable to formulate an etiological theory which applies to all cases. But this does not mean that research studies of individual cases are invalid or should be abandoned. We shall never understand these difficult people or help them to modify their behavior unless we are prepared to examine their life stories in detail and get to know them as persons.

It is only to be expected that research has been primarily directed toward the study of factors promoting antisocial behavior. It would be illuminating to turn this approach around and devote some attention to the factors—traits of character, positive assets, capabilities, personal relationships—which may be involved in *preventing* disadvantaged people from becoming antisocial. For example, we know that discharged prisoners who return to a stable family life are less likely to be reconvicted than those who lack such support. Studies of orphans and children who have been physically and sexually abused reveal that some suffer permanent damage, whilst others emerge, if not unscathed, at least able to lead relatively fruitful, rewarding lives. What has protected these children from being severely damaged? We do not know.

At the beginning of this chapter, I asked whether those manifesting antisocial personality disorders should be considered mentally ill, and raised the further question of whether they should be considered responsible for their antisocial behavior. These are questions which attorneys dealing with such cases often put to psychiatrists. I hope this chapter may have demonstrated why it is that such questions cannot be given precise answers. As we have seen, British law still refers to "psychopathic disorder" as "a persistent disorder or disability of mind"; and many states in the U.S. have legal provisions for dealing with psychopaths, in spite of the amorphous nature of this classification: "A 1950 New Jersey report cited twenty-nine different definitions of the condition by twenty-nine medical authorities."[18]

The newer definitions of the same group of abnormal personalities do not make the question of their legal status any easier to answer. It is clear that abnormality is not the same as illness, but not at all clear where abnormality begins and ends. For example, the term 'psychopath" has been applied to a variety of unusual individuals, some of whom have been highly successful. Some types of social deviance may be regarded as evidence of wickedness at one time and of illness at another.

> Much of what goes on in this process of redefining socially deviant activities as psychiatric is for strategic rather than scientific reasons. Public drunkenness, chronic alcoholism, and drug addiction were labeled as disease symptoms, as was homosexuality, in order to help the people charged with these offenses escape criminal punishment. Physicians and behavioral scientists publicly campaigned for a more humane approach to these and other conditions "in the name of mental health."[19]

59

Paradoxically, society's altruistic efforts to ensure that the sick get treated rather than punished have often meant involuntary confinement in mental institutions for indefinite periods rather than determinate prison sentences. Nicholas Kittrie's book *The Right to Be Different* gives many horrifying examples.

Many psychiatrists believe that there is no effective treatment for aggressive personality disorders. We have already noted that aggressive behavior tends to diminish with increasing age whether or not the individual is treated. Psychiatrists who specialize in such treatment usually agree that it requires long periods of exposure to programs designed to bring about social rehabilitation in special institutions. There are certainly some examples of habitually aggressive offenders who have mended their ways and proved capable of forming fruitful relationships. But one psychiatrist who has specialized in medico-legal matters writes:

> Most psychiatrists at present believe there is no effective treatment for psychopaths and so detaining them compulsorily is simply one method of solving the problems they cause for society in general. On the whole, psychopaths probably benefit from being dealt with under criminal and civil law, rather than mental health legislation.[20]

This may seem harsh to those who regard personality disorders as diminishing responsibility for crime. If a man "cannot help" behaving aggressively because he has an abnormal personality, it seems unjust to punish him. However, responsibility cannot be as accurately determined as lawyers would like it to be. When one man kills another because the voice of God has instructed him to do so, we say that he is mentally ill, acting under the influence of a delusion, and therefore not responsible for his actions. But most aggressive offenders do not exhibit delusions, hallucinations, thought disorder, or any other of the symptoms characteristic of definable mental illness. This is not to argue that such offenders are fully responsible. The more we learn about an individual's background, psychopathology, and motivation, the more difficult it becomes to decide which of his actions, whether good or bad, were inescapably determined by circumstance, and which were decided upon freely. Norval Morris, professor of law and criminology at the University of Chicago, has suggested that if mental illness is allowed as a defense which either diminishes criminal responsibility or entirely exculpates an offender, then other defenses are equally applicable.

> Why not a defense of "dwelling in a Negro ghetto"? This defense would not be morally indefensible. Such an adverse social and subcultural background is statistically *more* criminogenic than is psychosis, and it also severely circumscribes the freedom of choice which a nondeterministic criminal law (and that describes all present criminal law systems) attributes to accused persons.[21]

In our present state of knowledge, a pragmatic approach to these problems seems the only rational one to adopt. In the majority of cases, we cannot decide whether a man who has committed a crime is fully responsible or not. Society must be protected from habitually violent offenders; but whether they are confined in prisons or in mental hospitals should be a practical problem, not a moral one. Habitually violent offenders should usually be kept in prisons, because prisons are better equipped than hospitals to cope with them. If they require psychiatric treatment, they can be treated within the prison.

Complex, large societies will always contain a quota of people exhibiting the characteristic features of aggressive personality disorders. Because the causes of such abnormalities are multiple, we cannot hope entirely to abolish them. But this does not constitute an excuse for not doing as much as we possibly can to remedy the social evils which are known to contribute to habitually violent behavior. In the first chapter, I affirmed that the majority of people who commit violent acts in peacetime come from the bottom of the social heap, where many individuals feel humiliated, inadequate, ineffective, helpless, and inconsequential. Competitive, capitalist, industrial societies have not begun to solve, or even to address, the problem of making the less gifted and the less competent feel valued or wanted. If that problem could be solved, we can be sure that the prevalence of violent behavior would be substantially reduced.

# 3

---

# *Sadomasochism*

SADISM TAKES its name from the writings of the Marquis de Sade (1740–1814), masochism from those of the chevalier Leopold von Sacher-Masoch (1836–1895). A sadist may be defined as one who obtains sexual pleasure by inflicting pain, whilst a masochist gains sexual gratification from being cruelly treated or humiliated. The two forms of sexual behavior are usually described by the composite word "sadomasochism," because a person who becomes erotically aroused by either activity is also likely to be stimulated by its opposite. De Sade was primarily concerned with domination and the infliction of pain, whereas Sacher-Masoch wished to be

63

beaten and subjugated. But de Sade also had himself beaten, and Sacher-Masoch could be cruel. Objective studies confirm the link.

> Our statistical analysis, however, has revealed a very powerful sadomasochism factor that is unipolar rather than bipolar. Sadism and masochism do not seem to be opposites; instead they appear together in the same person or not at all. . . . Confirmation also comes from a study by Andreas Spengler (1977) of 245 members of German sadomasochistic clubs. Only a minority were orientated in an exclusively sadistic or masochistic direction; most of the men in the sample alternated between these two roles.[1]

It is also interesting to note that de Sade was fascinated by sodomy, whilst Sacher-Masoch had a fetishistic predilection for fur. So-called sexual deviations overlap and occur together fairly frequently.

The word "sadistic" is commonly misapplied to many violent acts, thereby creating the impression that cruelty and violence are often sexually motivated. The true sadist is a person who makes the infliction of pain and humiliation an integral part of obtaining sexual satisfaction. Fortunately, such people are rare. Violence and cruelty are not *primarily* sexual phenomena. When riot police use clubs to break the heads of unarmed students, they may find this exercise of power exhilarating, but it is unlikely that they experience erection or orgasm in the process. Even those trained as torturers are not usually sadists in the sense that they are sexually excited during torture, although a few may be. Most simply regard torture as a duty, a job which has to be done in the interests of the state, either in order to extract information or else as a means of terrorizing the populace.

Even so, there is a close link, at the physiological level, between aggressive arousal and sexual arousal. Ford and Beach write:

> The fact that many human societies implicitly recognize a connexion between sexual excitement and the infliction of pain upon one's partner is particularly interesting in view of the fact that fighting and mating are so closely related in a large number of vertebrate species. It is not an exaggeration to state that physically aggressive behaviour forms an integral part of the sexual pattern for vertebrates of every major phyletic class, although it does not follow that this is true of every species.[2]

And Melvin Konner notes:

> There is also evidence that some of the same conditions that might be expected to elicit fighting behavior can elicit male sexual behavior. For example, painful electric shock to a male rat will cause him to fight if he is in the presence of another male, but will enhance his sexual activity if he is in the presence of a female. Considering the many situations in nature in which males have to fight for the sex they want, this association is not surprising.[3]

The Kinsey team lists fourteen physiological changes common to the states of anger and sexual excitement. According to them, there are only four respects in which the physiology of sexual arousal differs from that of anger. Orgasm does not usually occur in anger; nor do erection and other manifestations of vasodilatation. (An angry person's face is likely to become "white with rage" as a result of vasoconstriction, though he may flush when the threat has passed.) The increased glandular secretion connected with the sexual organs is generally absent in anger; and so are the rhythmical muscular movements characteristic of sexual excitement. The Kinsey researchers point out that this close relation between the two states of arousal may explain why frustrated sexual responses so often turn into rage, or conversely, why anger, fighting, and quarrels may suddenly turn into sexual responses.[4] Subjectively, both states postpone fatigue and increase the individual's muscular tension and capacity, thus enhancing a sense of well-being and of vital participation in life. It is not surprising that adolescent males seek out situations like football games in which they become aggressively aroused, since such arousal is life-enhancing. Perhaps one reason "macho" displays and football violence are phenomena predominantly found amongst the young is that such activities, for individuals whose sexual life is not yet established, constitute alternative ways of seeking the excitement of physiological arousal.

Most murders should not be deemed sadistic, though there are a few instances of murderers experiencing sexual gratification during or shortly after the act of killing. Because such cases create considerable public interest and are widely reported, they appear to be more common than they are. Peter Kürten, the so-called Monster of Düsseldorf, admitted that he experienced orgasm when throttling or stabbing his victims.[5] Neville Heath, the pathological liar and false pretender mentioned in the last chapter, killed two women following sadistic sexual acts and was executed in 1946. John Christie, hanged in 1953 for the murder of six women in London, was a necrophiliac who seems to have been impotent with living women; he killed in order to use the dead body for sexual intercourse or masturbation.[6] The perpetrators of the "Moors Murders," Ian Brady and Myra Hindley, obtained sexual release in the course of ill-treating and murdering a number of children, whose corpses they buried on Saddleworth Moor.[7]

The general public tends to believe that such cases occur frequently, but objective research does not confirm this supposition. In an extensive study of sex offenders, the Kinsey team did not uncover any cases resembling the Moors Murders. "The murder of a child as an integral part of sexual gratification is a one-in-a-million phenomenon. We discovered no such murders, but a few of the aggressors vs. children whom we interviewed had inflicted injuries that might easily have led to death."[8] The majority of pedophiles, whether homosexual or heterosexual, do not employ violence when making sexual approaches to children. A minority use threats or enough force to achieve the required sexual contact; but severe injury to the child is uncommon. When child murders do occur, they are often the consequence of panic on the part of the adult, who may find himself strangling the child to stop it from screaming.

However, children are more easily dominated than adults and may thus especially appeal to the type of sadistic man who wants a helpless victim. Some cases of sexual abuse of children, especially those which are incestuous, are sadomasochistic. The child may be compelled to take part in rituals involving bondage, beating, and the like, and may be threatened with dire punishments if he or she does not comply. Because the child often dares not reveal the relationship, sexual abuse may go on for years without discovery. Since sexual abuse became a topic of discussion on television and radio, and since special telephone lines were made available for children to seek help, more cases have come to light. It is clear that until recently psychiatrists underestimated the prevalence of sexual abuse of children.

Peter Sutcliffe, the British multiple murderer known as "The Yorkshire Ripper," was found guilty of thirteen murders and seven attempted murders of women between 1975 and 1981. Although he sometimes inflicted savage injuries upon their sexual organs as well as other parts of their bodies, there seems no reason to suppose that he obtained sexual pleasure from these assaults. As a child, Sutcliffe was timid, shy, and habitually clung to his mother. He was embarrassed by anything to do with his body, avoided games, and clearly felt physically inadequate. He was ill at ease with sexually provocative girls, and when he eventually married, he chose a shy, withdrawn girl who had suffered an episode of schizophrenia. Sutcliffe's murders become partially comprehensible if one assumes that he was revenging himself upon the female sex, which he believed had humiliated him still more. Although he was not found to be mentally ill at his trial, he was eventually diagnosed as suffering from paranoid schizophrenia.[9]

Another multiple murderer, Dennis Nilsen, admitted killing at least fifteen young men. He ritually washed the dead bodies, made drawings of them, and described them as "beautiful" in his own voluminous writings. Although his choice of victims was determined by his homosexual orientation, and although he sometimes masturbated whilst gazing at the corpses, the act of murder itself was not associated with sexual excitement. Nor was Nilsen interested in causing pain. What he described was his pleasure in the chase. He used to select his victim, persuade him to come home, induce a "high" by a combination of alcohol and music, and then strangle him. Nilsen was primarily interested in power rather than in sex. He substituted the thrill of feeling omnipotent for the thrill of sexual orgasm. Nilsen was more intelligent and better educated than Sutcliffe but shared with him many of the personality traits characteristic of the multiple murderer. He was sentenced to life imprisonment in November 1983.[10]

Study of these individuals and what they say about themselves reveals that the desire for power and the desire for sex are inextricably mingled in varying proportions, but that the former generally takes precedence over the latter. According to Dr. Robert Brittain, the sadistic murderer is usually introspective, withdrawn, and predominantly solitary.[11] He is often a clinging "mother's boy" but may harbor intensely violent feelings toward his mother and other women which he is unable to express in any normal way. As a result, he lives a great deal in fantasy. He is often fascinated by pornography, by sadomasochistic films and videos, and by waxwork displays of the "chamber of horrors" variety. His actual sexual experience is generally very limited. He is often vain, meticulous about his appearance, and rather prim and proper, exhibiting obsessional concern with neatness. He is easily embarrassed and humiliated, and his offenses often follow upon some injury to his self-esteem. His murders have the effect of temporarily giving him a sense of superiority or of satisfying his need for revenge. The emotional release he achieves by murder is more a matter of experiencing a sense of godlike omnipotence than of taking delight in cruelty. He sometimes believes that he is so much cleverer than the police that he will escape conviction. In some instances, this fantasy is partially supported by the facts. Both Sutcliffe and Nilsen "got away with murder" for several years before they were detected. As we shall see, de Sade also had fantasies of omnipotence.

Similar conclusions apply to rape, in which the desire for sex and the desire for power or revenge are also mixed in varying proportions. In order to commit rape, the rapist has to be sexually aroused; but many rapists appear to be more interested in humiliating their victims and asserting their masculinity by means of violence than in obtaining sexual satisfaction. In a study of five hundred rapists, Groth estimated that forty percent were predominantly "anger" rapists. "The precipitating events were typically arguments, domestic problems, suspicions of infidelity, social rejections, and environmental frustrations. Common mediating emotions were a sense of anger and rage, associated with feelings of being wronged, hurt, put down and unjustly treated."[12] This type of rape commonly features more violence than is needed to produce compliance; and violence is often accompanied by verbal abuse, swearing, and acts calculated to degrade the victim.

Many rapes occur during the course of housebreaking. The offenders are usually young criminals who habitually use violence instrumentally to obtain what they want, whether it happens to be property or sexual satisfaction. Humiliation of the victim is not usually an integral component of such rapes. In other instances of rape, violence is minimal. Some rapists are men who think so poorly of themselves that they cannot believe any woman would willingly respond to their sexual advances. They therefore make threats of violence which they do not intend to put into practice, but which may be enough to secure the woman's submission. Sadistic murderers are rare; rape is all too common, although its true prevalence is hard to establish.

The issue of dominance versus submission and of the relative importance of sexuality and aggression in establishing dominance is not confined to man. In the first chapter, I discussed the adoption of conventions and rituals as ways of minimizing the destructiveness of conflicts between animals competing for the same resources. I also pointed out that animals who live in groups need to establish formal dominance relations in order to avoid damaging conflict with one another. The establishment of relatively fixed and recognizable hierarchies within a group of animals tends to prevent potential conflicts from becoming actual. If animal B is habitually submissive to animal A because the dominance of A has been previously established, fights between A and B become less likely. De Waal has described what he calls "the reconciled hierarchy model," in which he claims that "a well-recognised hierarchy promotes social bonds and reduces violence." In conflicts between animals, "the winner offers reconciliation and social tolerance in return for the loser's submission."[13] Formalization of this dominance-submission relation is established by rituals of various kinds, which can also be recognized in human interactions. Submissively presenting hindquarters or licking a dominant animal's neck is not psychologically far removed from the familiar ritual of saluting a superior officer.

In the first edition of *Social Psychology*, Roger Brown wrote:

The dominance order in many animal societies resembles a human status order in that it is also composed of inequalities of privilege and power. Dominance is like status also in its dependence upon individual differences and especially in its dependence upon age and sex. In dominance orders the male usually outranks the female and the mature animal the immature. This is also the usual way with human status orders. The determinants of male dominance beyond sex and age seem to be strength, aggressiveness, weaponry, fearsomeness of appearance, and ability to bluff. These things are not irrelevant to human status.[14]

He might have added that dominance in primates is also determined by the size of the individual's family and the number of his allies.

Such determinants are relevant to the study of sadomasochism. More than twenty-five years ago, Abraham Maslow and his co-workers asserted that much apparent sexual behavior, both in man and in nonhuman primates, was not what it appeared to be but was concerned more with aggression, status, dominance, and related concepts than with sensual pleasure or sexual satisfaction.[15] These varieties of behavior came to be called "pseudosexual."

What is particularly interesting in this context is that sexual behavior patterns are often employed in social interactions which determine rank order. This is true of both male and female behavior. In some species of monkeys and apes, sexual activity is initiated by females *presenting*. That is, the female approaches a male, turns her hindquarters toward him, and at the same time looks backward over her shoulder in his direction. There is a famous photograph of the film star Betty Grable adopting a similar pose. In some nonhuman primates, the invitation is underlined by the fact that the whole perineal area, including the genitals, becomes swollen and is often conspicuously colored when the animal is in heat. It has been demonstrated that the red color of the rump in rhesus monkeys is not itself a sexual signal, though it may increase the visibility of the female sexual swellings by contrast. It is not intensified, as are the sexual swellings, by the administration of sex hormones. Male rhesus monkeys are turned on sexually by smell rather than by sight. But the red rump does act "as a signal suppressing threat by an attacker."[16] Thus, in rhesus monkeys, "seeing red" has the opposite significance from that usually attributed to it in men and bulls.

It is not surprising that the gesture of presentation, in origin wholly sexual, becomes a means of indicating friendliness or submission, since it has the effect of suppressing aggression in the animal to which it is addressed. People who keep cats will recognize that when a cat greets her owner by rubbing against his legs, purring, and erecting her tail to display her ano-genital region, she is using presentation to indicate pleasurable recognition, friendship, and dependence.

In human beings, there are a number of conventional ways of indicating submission, including bowing, curtsying, kowtowing, and kneeling. These forms of behavior all make the submissive person appear smaller. Sadomasochistic rituals of real or simulated beating may involve one participant "bending over," thus adopting a posture closely similar to presentation in animals.

Although presentation is in origin a female gesture indicating readiness to mate, it can be used for nonsexual purposes by females at any stage of the estrus cycle, by young animals of either sex, and even by adult males. Presentation as a gesture of submission performed by both males and females in response to higher-ranking individuals has been described in many species of monkeys. In an interesting demonstration of presentation called "protected threat," if one monkey wants to attack another but dare not do so, he may threaten his opponent while presenting to a high-ranking male. This sometimes has the effect of persuading the dominant male to do the weaker monkey's fighting for him, just as a small boy at school may enlist the aid of a big boy to deal with a tormentor on his behalf.

Presentation is an example of a female sexual action which in purely social contexts has come to indicate submission or greeting. Male sexual actions can also be employed to indicate dominance or aggression in social settings. For example, Itani observed that a male macaque did not dare to take a tangerine which had landed between him and a higher-ranking male until the latter had reacted to the subordinate's presentation by mounting him.[17] Just as presentation, a female action, may be performed by either sex, so mounting, a male action, is performed by both sexes when dominance rather than coitus is in question. In some animals the testes usually descend into the scrotum only during courtship; this is true of the guinea pig, but it also uses this mechanism as a threat, displaying the descended testes to a rival when there is no question of copulation. Squirrel monkeys demonstrate dominance not by mounting but by thrusting the erect penis in another monkey's face. Females may use genital display for the same purpose. Penile display is sometimes used by males as a form of greeting.

Enough examples have been given to demonstrate that in animals other than man, sexual behavior patterns are habitually used for nonsexual, social purposes ranging from friendly greeting and the inhibition of threat and aggression to the establishment or affirmation of dominance-submission relationships. In the majority of examples of human sadistic behavior so far discussed, the establishment of dominance was seen to be more important than obtaining sexual release, although the two may be combined in some instances. Murder is the ultimate assertion of power by one human being over another; and we saw that rape is often an expression of rage rather than of sexual desire. Thus, a good deal of sadomasochistic behavior in man can justly be called "pseudosexual." It does not make sense, however, to call any form of animal behavior sadomasochistic. A cat playing with a mouse before killing it is not deliberately employing torture. The cat probably enjoys the exercise of its skill in catching and pouncing, but it cannot be supposed to gain pleasure from inflicting pain upon the mouse, since it is unable to appreciate the mouse's terror and distress. The human torturer or murderer may also derive enjoyment from the exercise of power; but it is surely his capacity to take pleasure in imagining what his victim is suffering which warrants the adjective "sadistic."

Human beings use sexual behavior patterns and sexual language in a variety of situations unconnected with sexuality itself. The Roman emperor Hadrian built a wall across the northern part of Britain as a barrier against marauding tribes of Picts and Scots. Much of this wall still survives. In one of the forts is a stone upon which an unmistakable phallus and testicles have been carved, pointing outward against potential intruders. "Fuck off" as a threat must date from the dawn of history. In ancient Athens, special types of sculpture consisting of square stone pillars surmounted by bearded heads and bearing an erect phallus and testicles in front were in common use as boundary markers or guards protecting houses and temples. The head was usually that of the god Hermes, and a statue of this kind was known as an ithyphallic Hermes.

Many readers will be familiar with Freud's statement in *The Interpretation of Dreams*: "All elongated objects, such as sticks, tree-trunks and umbrellas (the opening of these last being comparable to an erection), may stand for the male organ—as well as all long, sharp weapons, such as knives, daggers and pikes."[18] Freud always tried to reduce psychological processes to what he called an "indispensable organic foundation." This meant that he treated the genitals as an irreducible reality for which other things might be symbols or signs. He did not consider the opposite possibility: that the genitals might themselves signify something other than sexuality. Yet just as that phallic symbol a king's scepter indicates his royal power, so the penis itself, especially in ancient and franker times, was used as a symbol of authority or as a magical threat to ward off enemies.

This point was made succinctly by Jung, who supposedly remarked, "After all, the penis is only a phallic symbol."

The sexual offense known as "indecent exposure" is an example of employing the penis symbolically in a primitive attempt to gain recognition as a male by provoking shock or horror. The compulsion to "flash" the penis from a safe distance is one of the commonest sexual offenses, with just under two and a half thousand men convicted of it in Britain in 1975; the number of cases which are ignored or not prosecuted must be very much higher. Exhibitionists are often inhibited in their sexual relationships. They come predominantly from families in which the mother is the most powerful figure, and when they marry, they tend to be dominated by their wives. The compulsion to expose often occurs during times of marital stress or when the wife is pregnant. Most exhibitionists do not attempt closer contact with those to whom they expose themselves, and they usually pick young girls who are more likely to be shocked than sexually aroused. Some gain a modicum of satisfaction by masturbating after the act of exposure, but it is clear that exhibitionism is predominantly aggressive, more concerned with obtaining acknowledgment of power than with seeking sexual pleasure. According to one investigation, "The exhibitionists seem to have an inordinate need to please or to be appreciated by significant figures in their early lives. They had difficulty relating to the opposite sex, and often gave indications of covert hostility against females."[19] In this connection, it is pertinent to observe that the exhibitionist, by keeping his objects at a distance, may be protecting not only himself but also them from the possibility of attack. Exhibitionists, although heterosexual, are clearly ambivalent toward women.

The number of people who engage in sadomasochistic practices cannot be small, but actual prevalence is hard to determine. Flagellation is part of the stock-in-trade of many prostitutes, who may also supply racks, manacles, and other devices. In the last volume of *A la recherche du temps perdu*, Proust describes the narrator's visit to Jupien's brothel, where he witnesses the flogging of M. de Charlus with a whip studded with nails. Proust himself used to visit the original of this brothel, the Hôtel Marigny in Rue de l'Arcade in Paris. There is no evidence that Proust shared the Baron de Charlus's masochistic tastes, but he certainly combined a degree of sadism with his homosexuality. Proust liked to talk with handsome young men of working-class origin whom he supposed to be cruel or violent, persuading them to tell him about how they slaughtered animals and plunged their hands in blood. It is distressing to record that he also liked to watch young men pursue and destroy rats by hitting them with sticks or piercing them with hatpins.[20]

Throughout his life, the poet Swinburne was obsessed with flagellation and was an enthusiastic admirer of de Sade. He himself wrote extensively on the subject. From about the age of thirty, he was a frequent visitor to a brothel in St. John's Wood where flogging was on offer. His friend D. G. Rossetti thought his tastes degraded and made an attempt to cure him of his deviation by arranging for the American circus rider Adah Dolores Menken to seduce him. She seems not to have succeeded in this enterprise; for she is said to have returned the money Rossetti gave her, saying that ''she didn't know how it was, but she hadn't been able to get him up to the scratch, and couldn't make him understand that biting's no use.''[21] However, they became friends, and in spite of Swinburne's apparent impotence, Adah Menken was a frequent visitor to his rooms. Clad in flesh-colored tights and strapped to a horse, this sensational lady was famous for her portrayal of Mazeppa at Astley's Circus.

Swinburne's poem ''Dolores,'' which contains some of his best-known lines, is an impassioned hymn in praise of sadomasochism.

> Could you hurt me, sweet lips, though I hurt you?
>> Men touch them, and change in a trice
> The lilies and langours of virtue
>> For the roses and raptures of vice;
> Those lie where thy foot on the floor is,
>> These crown and caress thee and chain,
> O splendid and sterile Dolores,
>> Our Lady of Pain.

Swinburne imagined a past age in which Christianity had not yet imposed restraints upon sadomasochism.

> Thou wert fair in the fearless old fashion,
>> And thy limbs are as melodies yet,
> And move to the music of passion
>> With lithe and lascivious regret.

What ailed us, O gods, to desert you
    For creeds that refuse and restrain?
Come down and redeem us from virtue,
    Our Lady of Pain.

Sexual deviations originate in the imagination and flourish there much more luxuriantly than they do in reality, with which they often have only a tenuous connection. It is worth emphasizing the point that Proust, Swinburne, de Sade, and Sacher-Masoch were all novelists. Sacher-Masoch's novel *Venus in Furs* portrays the hero's mistress as a beautiful, cruel tyrant whose slave he is glad to be, and whose impossibly severe floggings he welcomes. Sacher-Masoch, who was professor of history at Graz, wrote, "When I was still a child I showed a predilection for the 'cruel' in fiction; reading this type of story would send shivers through me and produce lustful feelings. And yet I was a compassionate soul who would not have hurt a fly. . . . At the age of ten I already had an ideal woman."[22] Although Sacher-Masoch acted out his sexual preferences to some extent, it seems certain that his imagination took precedence.

The same applies to de Sade. Whereas Swinburne fantasized a fictitious past, de Sade imagined a future political regime in which every citizen would be free to engage in any sexual practice to which he was inclined. The marquis wrote most of his pornography—and his philosophy—while imprisoned in the Bastille or in the fortress of Vincennes. Although de Sade did act out his fantasies by ill-treating prostitutes, it is unlikely that we should be able to avail ourselves of the tedious possi-

81

bility of reading *Les 120 Journées de Sodome* or *La Nouvelle Justine* if he had not been confined in prison for eleven years. Simone de Beauvoir was surely right when she wrote:

> In choosing eroticism, Sade chose the make-believe. It was only in the imaginary that Sade could live with any certainty and without risk of disappointment. He repeated the idea throughout his work. "The pleasure of the senses is always regulated in accordance with the imagination." "Man can aspire to felicity only by serving all the whims of his imagination." It was by means of his imagination that he escaped from space, time, prison, the police, the void of absence, opaque presences, the conflicts of existence, death, life, and all contradictions. It was not murder that fulfilled Sade's erotic nature; it was literature.[23]

These authors are not the only writers to display sadomasochistic preoccupations. W. S. Gilbert's libretti for both *The Yeomen of the Guard* and *The Mikado* are overtly concerned with torture. Angus Wilson considers Rudyard Kipling's *Stalky and Co.* marred by "sadism disguised as moral realism."[24] Some of Conan Doyle's short stories, other than those about Sherlock Holmes, have sadomasochistic themes. Even Victorian literature for children contains barbaric scenes. Jack Harkaway, a best-selling hero during the last thirty years of the Victorian period, has adventures in which a man is gradually eaten alive and a girl is tortured with red-hot stones.

Sadomasochistic interests are not confined to a small minority of human beings. The Kinsey team found that twenty-two percent of their male sample and twelve percent of their female sample reported some arousal from sadomasochistic stories.[25] When they later came to examine sex offenders, they discovered that "of the sex offenders whose offenses included violence or duress, between one eighth and one fifth reported arousal from sadomasochistic noncontact stimuli."[26] If we add to these figures the large number of males who are aroused by fetish objects suggesting sadomasochistic relationships, such as high heels, boots, and tight clothing, we are forced to conclude that some degree of interest in sadomasochism is practically universal. Chinese footbinding, hobble skirts, and similar restrictive devices recur throughout the history of fashion. They attest the eagerness with which men welcome the partial crippling of women as a way of making them appear more helpless. The submissiveness with which women have followed many uncomfortable or partially immobilizing fashions may be taken as evidence of their wish to please men. On the other hand, as Beatrice Faust points out, such fashions may also give pleasure to women themselves: "High heels and corsets provide intense kinaesthetic stimulation for women, appealing to the sense of touch but extending more than skin deep. These frivolous accessories are not just visual stimuli for men: they are also tactile stimuli for women."[27]

The Kinsey team originally concluded that women show much less interest than men in psychosexual stimuli of every kind and also appear to be less susceptible than men to sexual conditioning.

We have, then, thirty-three bodies of data which agree in showing that the male is conditioned by sexual experience more frequently than the female. The male more often shares, vicariously, the sexual experiences of other persons, he more frequently responds sympathetically when he observes other individuals engaged in sexual activities, he may develop stronger preferences for particular types of sexual activity, and he may react to a great variety of objects which have been associated with his sexual activities. The data indicate that in all of these respects, fewer of the females have their sexual behavior affected by such psychologic factors.[28]

Later research has thrown doubt on some of these findings, which may be determined more by culture than by innate biological differences. Women exposed to erotica may respond physically but are more likely than men to deplore their own reactions. Intense sexual arousal may lead both men and women to scratch, bite, or pinch their sexual partners, and some find that such mildly painful stimuli increase their excitement. I have treated one woman who was alarmed by the severity of the bruising inflicted by her lover, which she herself had invited.

But most sadomasochistic sexual practices do not cause much physical injury or pain. Indeed, some psychologists who have made a particular study of sadomasochism call for redefinition of this type of sexual behavior, on the grounds that many sadomasochistic practices involve no real elements of pain, humiliation, or restriction. Gosselin and Wilson claim that the classic definitions of sadomasochism are somewhat meaningless in reality, because neither party in a sadomasochistic partnership really regards the agreed form of pain as anything more than arousal, humiliation as anything more than the joyous right to adore or be adored, and restriction as anything more than permission to be still, to give in or even to release aggression without fear of hurting anyone.[29]

The authors define what they believe to be the most prevalent form of sadomasochism as follows:

A relationship giving rise to the sexual interaction of two or more people via a ritual whose outward appearance involves coercion, pain, restriction or suffering of some kind but which has been agreed upon, tacitly or overtly, between the parties concerned and may in reality involve none of these constraints.[30]

So sadomasochism is not what it seems. When it is "acted out" in murder and rape, the dimension of power, of dominance versus submission, is more important than the dimension of sex. The same is true of the much commoner forms of sadomasochism, fantasies or rituals which do not involve pain or injury. To illustrate the point that total submission is the primary concern of the masochist and that pain is secondary or incidental, I quote from the fantasies of a male masochist, now deceased.

I like to imagine any group of men or women being led into slavery. Slave markets. Being stripped naked, examined as animals. Being sold, having a master to work for or submit to sexually.

A master is superior to God because he exists in the flesh. A slave realizes that he is significant only so far as he is perfectly submissive. He delights in his status as slave and loves seeing others enslaved. Two chief moments of pleasure in the fantasies. 1. The moment of enslavement. Free one minute, slave the next. This is the recurring importance of the slave market scenes. I ought to add that in my mind it has a kind of poetic beauty. 2. The moment they are possessed by their master. Their life has been empty and without meaning, frivolous and trivial. Now it is exactly the opposite.

A slave has no past, he has no name. A master is beyond criticism, whatever he does or orders is immensely significant, he is incapable of evil or wrong, he cannot insult or degrade a slave. He can only honour him by noticing him. The only relationship the slave fears is that of friendship. This would be against nature and shatter his world.[31]

It is interesting to contrast this picture with its opposite. De Sade wrote a novel called *Aline and Valcour* in which he depicted his own childhood and fantasies of his own omnipotence.

Allied through my mother with all the grandest in the kingdom, and connected through my father with all that was most distinguished in Languedoc—born in Paris in the heart of luxury and plenty—as soon as I could think I concluded that nature and fortune had joined hands to heap their gifts on me. This I thought because people were stupid enough to tell me so, and that idiotic presumption made me haughty, domineering and ill-tempered. I thought that everything should give way before me, that the entire universe should serve my whims, and that I merely needed to want something to be able to have it.[32]

The sheer volume of sadomasochistic pornography attests the fact that sadomasochistic interests are widespread in Western society. Pornographic bookshops are stocked with magazines detailing flagellation, bondage, and sexual coercion. There is a large subterranean industry which produces films and video cassettes explicitly portraying sadomasochistic scenes. Most of these are nasty, brutish, and vulgar; but *Salò*, the last film made by the famous Italian director Pasolini, which is based on de Sade's *Les 120 Journées de Sodome*, is an exception. Although it has been described as "ruthlessly and almost unwatchably repellent," some consider it a masterpiece.[33] When police search the homes of sexual offenders, they sometimes discover collections of pornography. But the possession or consumption of pornography does not distinguish those who are likely to commit sexual offenses from those who are not. Most authorities agree that people who collect pornography are following preexisting interests. There is no evidence that pornography contributes to the commission of offenses or that it creates sexual interests which were not there previously.

According to Steven Marcus, the rise of pornography is inseparable from the rise of the novel.[34] Pornography originated in the seventeenth century, became well established in the eighteenth, flourished in the nineteenth, and continues to flourish today. Some authorities reckon that as much as eighty percent of pornography is sadomasochistic. There was an extraordinary efflorescence of flagellation pornography during the Victorian period, which is examined in Marcus's *The Other Victorians*.

Pornographic writing, whether or not concerned with sadomasochism, is usually crude, badly composed, and repetitive; but here again there are some exceptions. John Cleland's novel *Fanny Hill*, first published in the eighteenth century, is elegantly written. It is mostly devoted to straightforward sexual intercourse, but it does contain a scene in which one of Fanny's clients requires her to whip him and then whips her in order to reach sexual fulfillment.[35]

The modern *Histoire d'O*, by a pseudonymous author, is principally concerned with flagellation but is claimed to have literary merit.[36] Although the book is supposed to have been written by a woman, it is primarily a fantasy of male dominance. O is taken to a mysterious château where she is whipped, chained, and made to submit to the sexual attentions of a series of men. She is not allowed any independence, not even the freedom of her own body. Her clothes, makeup, demeanor, and occupation are all dictated by the whim of the master to whom she is assigned. It is no accident that she is known as O; for she is nothing in her own right, merely a product of male fantasy. O is alleged to enjoy her total submission, but there is little emphasis on sexual pleasure. What she is supposed to gain is a sense of her own significance as a participant in a greater reality, that of her ruthless master. Her story is closely parallel with the fantasy of the slave market quoted above. Although the sexually mature person may not share such fantasies, many have experienced the "oceanic" feeling of merging with a reality greater than themselves, be it the Deity, Nature, or the experience of music or painting. As Fenichel put it:

> Certain narcissistic feelings of well-being are characterised by the fact that they are felt as a reunion with an omnipotent force in the external world brought about either by incorporating parts of this world, or by the fantasy of being incorporated by it. Religious ecstasy, patriotism, and similar feelings are characterised by the ego's participation in something unattainably high.[37]

But such participation is at the expense of identity. It reduces the individual to a cipher, making a person into nothing but an O. Sadomasochistic fantasy is indeed narcissistic, in that one sexual partner is made to serve the needs of the other and thus disappears as a separate person whose own needs have to be taken into account. In fantasy there is no conception of mutuality, of pleasure exchanged and shared on equal terms; although in real relationships there is often mutuality.

Why are sadomasochistic fantasies so common? As we have noted, sexual deviations originate in the imagination—a curious, distorted reflection of man's unique capacity to transcend the physical. Sexual fantasies become particularly insistent in the imaginations of people who are in some way alienated from their bodies and are consequently prevented from achieving sexual fulfillment in straightforward physical lovemaking. In societies which are tolerant of sexual interests and sexual play between children, and which make no secret of adult sexual behavior, any form of sexual deviation or sexual inhibition is uncommon. As mentioned earlier, minor forms of aggressive scratching or biting occur universally; but sadomasochism, in the sense of deliberately inflicting or receiving pain or engaging in rituals connected with dominance and submission, seems not to be found in preliterate societies. Sexual deviations are chiefly the product of complex Western societies in which negative attitudes to sexuality produce guilt, inhibition, and uncertainty about personal attractiveness and effectiveness. In such societies, many people have difficulty forming the kind of interpersonal relationships in which sexual love can be freely given and received on equal terms.

Steven Marcus makes the interesting suggestion that sadomasochistic preoccupations are compensatory phenomena.

If pornography in general amounted to a reversal of Victorian moral ideals, then the literature of flagellation represented a reversal of Victorian ideal personal standards for men. The striking features of this literature are its childishness, extreme incoherence, absence of focus, confusion of sexual identity, and impulse toward play-acting or role-playing. These qualities stand in marked contrast to the Victorian ideals of manliness, solidity, certitude of self, straightforwardness, sincerity and singleness of being. Yet by now, I think, it would be something of a surprise if we were to find that such ideals were not, in a culture, accompanied somewhere by their opposite—the very strength with which those ideals were enforced and striven for tended to ensure, or even to necessitate, the existence of such formations as the literature of flagellation.[38]

But if sadomasochistic interests were wholly phenomena of compensation, we should expect that a decline in such interests would have taken place during the last fifty years, *pari passu* with the diminished emphasis upon Victorian ideals of masculinity and the general permissiveness characteristic of our era. No such decline has occurred. Sadomasochistic literature continues to be produced in huge quantities, no doubt, as Marcus suggests, partly for compensatory reasons, though what is being compensated is not simply the Victorian ideal of masculinity but a complex series of Western attitudes toward sex which go back centuries. Sadomasochism and other types of deviant sexual behavior seem to be ways of circumventing prohibitions: symbolic expressions of sexuality, or rituals which generate sexual arousal in an indirect fashion, thus overcoming the blocks to arousal by direct, simple physical stimuli. Sadomasochistic fantasies are unwillingly entertained by a variety of highly respectable people who would never act upon them and are sometimes deeply distressed by them. A compulsive interest in flagellation or bondage is often felt as a horrifying preoccupation by sensitive people and may drive them to seek psychiatric help.

Today most Western-educated people feel that ideally human lovemaking should contain no elements of dominance and submission; that it should be a mutual exchange of pleasure and fulfillment on equal terms, in which neither partner feels coerced by the other. Sadomasochistic behavior is rightly considered deviant or immature, though it is arguable that some minor elements of domination and submission can be detected in even the most mature sexual encounters. It used to be conventionally expected that the human male should initiate sexual activity, even though the female may have indicated her readiness by dressing or behaving seductively. The conformation of the genitals and the act of coitus itself demand active penetration on the part of the male, whereas the female can remain relatively passive and receptive if she wishes. There is some correlation between dominance and masculinity, and between submissiveness and femininity, as studies of sexual fantasy have demonstrated. Women do not rape; and by far the majority of crimes involving violence are committed by men.

In clinical psychiatric practice, male patients can be either sadistic or masochistic, and many are both. But whilst it is fairly common to see masochistic women who want to be subjugated or even physically ill-treated as a prelude to sexual arousal, it is rare to encounter women who want to behave sadistically to men in order to secure sexual satisfaction for themselves. This is not to deny that women can be aggressive to men. Some nag unmercifully in the hope that the man will finally treat them with the force they find exciting. Others, preferring power to pleasure, use their sexuality as a means of asserting dominance. Although her male victims often become emotional casualties, the *femme fatale* is not unknown in psychiatric practice.

The type is archetypally portrayed by Princess Turandot, heroine of Puccini's opera. As convention demands, Turandot is endowed with great beauty. The man who wins her also wins the imperial throne of China, so to be sure that he is worthy of such an honor, a test is contrived. The aspirant suitor must give correct answers to three riddles. If he fails, he is put to death. The intrepid prince of Tartary who dares to woo her answers the first two riddles correctly. The last riddle put by Turandot to Calaf is: "What is the ice which sets you on fire?" The answer is Turandot herself, the ice-cold *femme fatale* who cannot love. The first psychotic woman I ever saw complained that her vagina contained a block of ice, a delusion expressing truth by means of a similar metaphor. It is only when Turandot passes beyond her sadomasochistic concern with domination that she is able to melt in the arms of her new lover.

In clinical practice, every psychiatrist will have encountered women like Turandot. Freud interpreted their behavior as "penis envy"; but I think it more likely that their insistence on domination conceals a fear that any intimate encounter with a male will be hurtful or cause injury.

Freud pointed out that children who observe the

"primal scene" of sexual intercourse between their parents or other adults often interpret it as an attack by the male upon the female. In some people, such early experiences may reinforce the link between patterns of sexual behavior and patterns of dominance-submission. Sexual arousal and aggressive arousal may also be more persistently linked in those who have learned as children to associate physical closeness to others with pain and punishment rather than tenderness and affection. Such people cannot trust others not to hurt them in situations of intimacy which make them vulnerable. As a result, they may adopt an aggressive, dominant stance in which sexual intercourse is treated as "screwing" or "fucking" rather than as an expression of love.

It is surely natural that children should sometimes misinterpret the sexual act as an attack. In spite of infantile masturbation, children have little idea what is involved in adult sexual intercourse. But they do have a lively concept of dominance-submission relationships, being perpetually engaged in struggles to establish status in relation to their parents, in rivalry with siblings and contemporaries, and in all the manifold fantasies so characteristic of the childhood wish to be as big, as strong, and as powerful as the adults on whom they are dependent.

Freud originally thought that sadism was part of the sexual instinct itself. I think this view has led to a mistaken emphasis upon the sexual aspects of sado-masochism as opposed to its significance in terms of power relations. Freud wrote:

The sexuality of most male human beings contains an element of *aggressiveness*—a desire to subjugate; the biological significance of it seems to lie in the need for overcoming the resistance of the sexual object by means other than the process of wooing. Thus sadism would correspond to an aggressive component of the sexual instinct which has become independent and exaggerated and, by displacement, has usurped the leading position.[39]

I am not convinced by this explanation, because I do not share Freud's view that women have such a resistance to sex that they have to be vanquished by means other than wooing. It took the World War of 1914—18 to convince Freud that he must recognize aggression as separate from sex. If Freud had had the opportunity to study animal behavior and had recognized the significance of dominance and submission at an earlier stage in his thinking, he might have formulated his theories of sadomasochism differently. The emphasis of conventional psychoanalysis has always been upon infantile *sexuality*, and upon the extent to which the persistence of infantile sexual constellations interferes with the establishment of adult genitality. I think it more likely that the chief difficulty children encounter is in establishing a sense of their own power and status in the familial and social hierarchy, and that their sexual difficulties are secondary to this rather than primary. This interpretation is also relevant to the behavioral differences between the sexes referred to above.

Karen Horney was one of the first women psychoanalysts to attack Freud's concept of penis envy: "An assertion that one half of the human race is discontented with the sex assigned to it and can overcome this discontent only in favorable circumstance—is decidedly unsatisfying, not only to feminine narcissism, but also to biological science."[40] Karen Horney is certainly right; but if we take penis envy as *pseudosexual* rather than sexual, we can give Freud's clinical observation a different interpretation.

It is not that the immature girl is dissatisfied with being female but that, like all children, she resents being comparatively powerless. In her quest for status, she encounters the fact that boys, for the most part, are both stronger and more aggressive than girls, and that in adult life, males are socially dominant in all existing human societies. We may deplore this, but we cannot dispute it. As we noted earlier, primitive symbols of masculine power are undoubtedly phallic. It may be pedantic to use the term "phallic envy" rather than "penis envy"; but the substitution underlines the distinction I am suggesting. As long as the child or the childish adult feels at a disadvantage in the dominance hierarchy, so long will both sexes display phallic envy, tend to identify with the more powerful male, and show traces of pseudosexual sadomasochistic behavior.

The more neurotic a person is, the more will he or she be preoccupied with status and feelings of weakness or inferiority. The human child, compared with the young of other species, takes a long time to grow up. During this prolonged period of immaturity, the child is under the protection of, and dominated by, persons who are older, bigger, and more powerful. It is not surprising that some people, even when physically mature, lack confidence and continue to regard their peers as more "grown up" and hence more powerful than themselves. Such people may be unable to give or receive love on equal terms and thus may have to assert dominance before they can enjoy sexual activities.

Paradoxically, the masochistically inclined exhibit a similar attitude toward others but deal with it in the opposite fashion. Masochistic submission implicitly includes permission to behave sexually from the partner who is required to adopt the dominant role. The master or mistress takes charge; and so the subordinate participant is relieved of guilt and responsibility for his sexuality. Some masochistic rituals involving punishment are devices which allow the guilty subject to "sin" again because he has expiated his previous sins by his pain. It seems probable that the severe beatings to which T. E. Lawrence ("Lawrence of Arabia") submitted at his own instigation served this function amongst others.[41]

Submission to a dominant partner makes it possible for some inhibited, guilty people to experience orgasm when they would otherwise find it difficult to do so. Obsessional personalities find it hard to "let go" in a variety of situations. If control is handed over to an external authority, the severity of the subject's superego may be temporarily modified and the ecstatic release of orgasm finally secured.

Total submission to another is a regression to the state of a helpless child; but it is generally a submission in which the other is required to behave in certain specified ways, and is therefore an indirect form of domination. Sacher-Masoch's heroine Wanda is described as dominant and cruel, but when she treats Severin like a slave, she is actually complying with his own requests. Children, paradoxically, are powerful because of their helplessness, as everyone who has looked after a baby must recognize; and adults who feel in need of help or protection often behave childishly for this reason.

The links between sexual behavior and aggressive or violent behavior are complex; but I hope that this chapter has established that violence and cruelty cannot be regarded as *primarily* sexual, and that sadomasochism is more pseudosexual than sexual. Part of the confusion which has muddied our understanding of these forms of behavior must be laid at Freud's door, for Freud equated pleasure with sexual pleasure, even alleging that the pleasure we take in beauty is no more than a sublimated derivative of the sexual drive. In his book *Jokes and Their Relation to the Unconscious*, Freud dismissed joy in the overcoming of difficulties or joy in power as invariably secondary phenomena. Freud's attitude to power may in part reflect his repudiation of Alfred Adler, who was one of the first major dissenters amongst the early psychoanalysts. In Adler's view, self-assertion and the will to power took precedence over sex as the prime mover of human conduct. Freud treated Adler's disagreement with him as heresy and may have blinded himself to the significance of power in human relationships on this account.

Yet who can doubt that power and pleasure in its exercise are fundamental sources of satisfaction? This is evident at every level in society. The petty official engaged in "welfare" work may experience little pleasure in being helpful but all too often enjoys humiliating clients to whom he feels superior. The dictator who can sway multitudes with his oratory, or uproot whole populations and put to death all opponents, clearly relishes his position. For many natures, the pleasures of exercising power are more compelling than those of sex, which is perhaps one reason why the home lives of so many politicians seem unsatisfactory.

I shall argue that human violence and cruelty are predominantly concerned with power relationships. Although the study of aggressive personality disorders and sadomasochism throws some light upon these distasteful aspects of human nature, we must turn our attention to the question with which this book began. How is it that so-called "normal" people can be persuaded to treat their fellows with barbarous cruelty?

# 4

## The Ubiquity of Paranoia

IN THE first chapter, we saw that many species of animals have adopted rituals and conventions which generally prevent aggressive behavior from becoming lethal, although we also noted that intraspecific killing is now known to occur more often than zoologists had previously supposed. Although some remnants of ritualized inhibition can be detected in man, human beings are exceptionally destructive. It has been calculated that no fewer than 59,000,000 individuals perished between 1820 and 1945 as the result of war, murder, or other lethal activities.[1] This immense slaughter cannot be explained in the same terms we use to interpret the destructive behavior of rival groups of insects and rodents. Differences between human beings, such as color, smell, and physical appearance, can be underlined and used as propaganda to create or aggravate hostility between groups or individuals, but a great deal of human violence and cruelty occurs between people who cannot be distinguished from each other by such criteria. Compared with other animals, supposedly "civilized" man is peculiar in being particularly destructive and cruel to his own species.

Some of the factors which account for this peculiarity have been touched on in the preceding chapters. It is well established that a cruel or neglectful upbringing is likely to produce an adult who behaves accordingly. Common factors in family violence include "a misperception of the victim, low self-esteem, sense of incompetence, social isolation, a lack of support and help, lack of empathy, marital difficulties, depression, poor self-control, and a history of abuse or neglect as a child."[2] Physical abuse of children is a particularly disturbing and repellent form of violence. In general, small size and weakness evoke protective, tender responses, both in humans and in animals. If this were not so, the young would not survive. Yet physical abuse of children is very common. In Britain, the National Society for the Prevention of Cruelty to Children reported 9,500 cases of physical abuse and 6,350 cases of sexual abuse in 1986. The Society believes that at least 200 children a year die as a result of maltreatment by their parents.[3] Parents

who batter their children were generally battered themselves, and research has disclosed a pattern of three
generations of abuse in some families.[4]

Many normal parents have experienced temporary
frustration when faced with a baby who will not stop
crying, but any anger they may feel is usually overridden by concern for the baby's distress. Parents who
habitually feel ineffectual because of their own childhood deprivation may regard the baby's crying as an
added demonstration of their inadequacy and hence
respond with violence. Some parents demand from
their children the affection they were not given when
they themselves were children, becoming resentful if
the child is unable to fulfill their needs by being constantly affectionate and responsive. Others require instant obedience and feel that their own self-esteem is
threatened if the child does not immediately comply
with their orders. Many assaults on small children are
perpetrated by drunken fathers or stepfathers. Some are
carried out by parents or stepparents who are themselves scarcely more than children. Two examples, reported on the same day in the same newspaper, are
unfortunately typical.

> An unemployed man began a sustained assault on his
> five-year-old daughter Sukina after she refused to spell
> her name for him, Bristol Crown Court was told yes-
> terday.
>    The beating, by David Hammond, with a ruler,
> plastic tubing, fists and a kettle flex resulted in her death
> from multiple injuries, the prosecution alleged. . . .

Miss Kent [the girl's mother] said there was nothing she could do. "Sukina had cried so much she couldn't cry any more." The beating was so severe the girl was unable to get up at her father's command. "He picked her up by the hair and carried her up the stairs," she said.

There Mr. Hammond chucked the girl fully clothed into the bath.

Danny Palmer, the teenager accused of battering to death his seven-month-old stepson, watched cartoons on television as the baby lay dying in hospital, an Old Bailey jury heard yesterday. . . . The court has heard that Christopher died from three heavy blows to his head, causing multiple fractures and brain damage. . . . The prosecution claims the fatal injuries may have been inflicted by a rounders bat, found concealed in the baby's bedroom. A post-mortem examination also showed he had extensive bleeding in both eyes, both arms had been snapped just above the wrists and his mouth was torn.[5]

Ill-treatment of small children is one example of how a human being who is in fact powerless can yet be perceived as threatening. One of the most unpleasant features of human violence is that it is often employed upon a victim who is entirely helpless and at the mercy of the attacker. This is seldom the case in other species. In ritualized contests between animals, the loser will often signal his defeat by presenting a vulnerable part of his anatomy to the winner. This has the effect of inhibiting further attack, and the loser is generally allowed to go free. In contrast, human beings frequently torture and humiliate their defeated enemies for reasons which will be further explored below.

A second important factor facilitating the employment of violence and cruelty by normal people is the human tendency toward obedience. In the first chapter, it was briefly pointed out that animals which live in groups need to form hierarchies if peace is to be preserved between individuals, and that obedience to high-ranking animals is required if the group is to be rapidly moved in order to protect it from predators. In recent years, researchers have emphasized the fact that the establishment of stable hierarchies lessens aggressive interactions and fosters cooperative bonds. In man, as in other social animals, obedience is adaptive. Social life would be impossible if there was no system of authority, and no general tendency to obey that authority. Most people automatically obey the directions of an usher in a theater or a policeman on the street; and chaos would result if they did not. If a group of individuals is to act together, it must obey the commands of a leader. Musicians usually find that when an ensemble contains ten players or more, a conductor becomes necessary to ensure synchronization.

But behavior which is adaptive in one setting can be maladaptive in another. Becoming part of a hierarchy inevitably involves the partial abandonment of individual decision-making and control. The restraints usually imposed by conscience when an individual is acting independently are *necessarily* impaired directly when he becomes part of a hierarchical social structure.

In wartime, governmental authority overrides the usual prohibitions about killing one's fellow men, and it becomes a duty to slaughter those whom the government has labeled enemies. How far obedience to authority exculpates an individual who has committed evil acts is still an unsolved moral problem and has been a matter of philosophical dispute since the time of Plato. Conservative philosophers argue that disobedience so threatens the structure of society that it is better to carry out evil acts prescribed by government than run the risk of anarchy. Liberal humanists affirm the sovereignty of the individual conscience and condemn those who have executed cruel orders even when refusal to do so would have entailed death. It is easy for armchair moralists in peacetime to condemn violence and cruelty committed during the stress of war or under duress from a higher authority. Military training insists that obeying orders is the first duty of the soldier. There are striking examples of exceptionally brave individuals who have refused to carry out brutal orders, but we can never be sure how we ourselves would behave in similar circumstances. In military settings, the soldier who obeys orders is described as being loyal and "doing his duty," so that disobedience appears morally reprehensible as well as a dangerous infringement of military discipline. Many who took part in the horrors of the concentration camps disowned responsibility for what they did. Even those who were proven to have been grossly cruel defended their actions in terms of obedience. When the notorious Nazi torturer Irma Grese was taxed with cruelty, she said defiantly, "It was our duty to exterminate antisocial elements, so that Germany's future should be assured."

It is clear that Stanley Milgram's famous experiments on obedience were prompted by revelations of what went on in the Nazi concentration camps, of which there were over thirty, each requiring a large staff of guards. It is conservatively estimated that at least 5,000,000 Jews were exterminated in these camps. This figure takes no account of the attempted genocide of other groups: Poles, Russians, and Gypsies. When the gas chambers and crematoria at Auschwitz were in full operation, 6,000 victims a day were systematically slaughtered. The scale of these operations and the administrative structure supporting them required the employment and cooperation of thousands of individuals. Although a few sociopaths or sadists may have welcomed the opportunities such work afforded them, the majority of those employed in the camps must, by definition, be regarded as normal, ordinary human beings.

Milgram's experiments go some way toward demonstrating how it comes about that average citizens can be persuaded to participate in horror. Since Milgram's work is well known, I shall summarize it only briefly.

A person comes to a psychological laboratory and is told to carry out a series of acts that come increasingly into conflict with conscience. The main question is how far the participant will comply with the experimenter's instructions before refusing to carry out the actions required of him.[6]

107

The volunteers participating in the experiment are told that they are taking part in a study designed to investigate the effect of punishment upon learning. They are shown a "learner" seated in a chair, his arms strapped to prevent much movement, and an electrode attached to his wrist. The learner is told that he has to learn a list of word pairs, and that when he makes an error, he will receive an electric shock which will increase in intensity with each mistake. The volunteer participant is then taken into the next room and seated before a generator which will give shocks ranging from 15 volts to 450 volts. The switches have labels ranging from "Slight Shock" to "Danger—Severe Shock." The "teacher" is told that when the learner makes a mistake, he is to give him an electric shock. He is to start at the lowest level, but at each mistake he is to increase the severity of the shock until he reaches the highest level. The learner, an actor who in fact receives no shocks at all, is trained to show increasing levels of distress, grunting at 75 volts, overtly complaining at 120 volts, and demanding to be released at 150 volts. At 285 volts his response is described as "an agonized scream."

Although many of the participants in the experiment showed signs of unease and conflict about inflicting pain on another human being, almost two-thirds proved to be obedient subjects, and a substantial proportion continued to the last shock on the generator, in spite of their belief that they were causing severe distress or even endangering the life of the learner.

In one variant of the experiment, the learner is

instructed to reveal that he has "a slight heart condition" and to express anxiety about the effect of electric shocks. After he is reassured by the experimenter that the shocks do not cause permanent tissue damage although they may be painful, the experiment proceeds. At 150 volts the learner begs to be released, but the experimenter insists on proceeding. In spite of the learner's agonized protests, including complaints that his heart is being affected, 26 of 40 subjects continue to the end and administer the maximum shock of 450 volts.

Although a psychologist conducting laboratory experiments at a respected university has a certain authority, it is far less than a commanding officer exercises in wartime, backed by the power to institute court-martials and order punishments. Milgram himself was surprised and dismayed by how far ordinary individuals would go in complying with the experimenter's orders. Subjects interviewed after the experiments repeatedly said, "I wouldn't have done it by myself. I was just doing what I was told."[7] Milgram comments:

> It is the old story of "just doing one's duty" that was heard time and time again in the defense statements of those accused at Nuremberg. But it would be wrong to think of it as a thin alibi concocted for the occasion. Rather, it is a fundamental mode of thinking for a great many people once they are locked into a subordinate position in a structure of authority. The disappearance of a sense of responsibility is the most far-reaching consequence of submission to authority.[8]

109

The film *Your Neighbour's Son* is an accurate recon-
struction of the methods used in Greece to train torturers when the junta of the colonels was in power. First
a selection was made of young men thought to be sym-
pathetic to the regime, or at any rate right-wing, most of
them from rural areas. They were told that they had
been specially chosen to be members of an elite group
which would carry out important duties on behalf of
their country. They were then taken to camps where
they were subjected to extremes of physical punishment
and humiliation, which they were told was necessary
training in toughness. Instant obedience to orders, however irrational, was demanded. Thus, recruits were
wakened at any hour of the night and drilled; made to
eat grass or burning cigarette butts; forced to crawl to
the canteen on their knees; or made to perform exercises carrying heavy equipment until they were physically exhausted. Failure to show instant obedience
resulted in beatings. As one recruit said, "We were
made to love pain."

Gradually they were introduced to torture; first by
witnessing it, and then by participating in the beating of
prisoners. Any attempt to help prisoners was severely
punished, and reluctance to participate in torture was
dismissed as "sissy." Recruits were given special uni-
forms and privileges not available to the general public.
They were taught to think of themselves as a special
corps of military police which ordinary people would
both esteem and fear. In El Salvador, the regime has
required secret police to torture and interrogate political
prisoners suspected of being left-wing guerrillas. Sim-

ilarly punitive methods of training potential recruits have been reported.

Recruits trained in this fashion came to regard torture of suspected dissidents as a duty and were proud of performing this duty efficiently. There is no reason to suppose that these men gained pleasure from torturing others. To them it became simply a job which had to be done. Twenty-five Greek torturers who were interviewed after the fall of the junta were leading normal lives; and after periods of observation varying from six to ten years, only one of the twenty-five showed any evidence of guilt or remorse.

In a review of Hannah Arendt's book on Eichmann, the psychiatrist Bruno Bettelheim, who was himself a prisoner in both Dachau and Buchenwald, discusses compliance and how far it is possible to assert individual values in a totalitarian state. Eichmann was not a monster but an obedient civil servant. The subtitle of Arendt's book on his trial is *A Report on the Banality of Evil*.[9] However, Bettelheim claims that there is usually a definable point when the individual makes a choice which proves irrevocable.

This moment of choice came when Eichmann for the very first time visited the extermination camps and saw what happened to the Jews. He nearly fainted. But instead of heeding his emotional reaction, he pushed it down to go on with the task that he had been assigned and that he embraced as his own obligation. This was Eichmann's point of no return. Then and there he abdicated from reacting as a human being and made himself

111

a mere tool of the state. . . . My thesis is that if one does not stand up to one's experience in accordance with one's values, if one takes the first step in cooperating with the totalitarian system at the expense of one's convictions and sentiments, one is caught in a web that tightens with each step of cooperation until it becomes impossible to break free.[10]

The Holocaust is undoubtedly this century's most horrific example of mass extermination preceded by utmost cruelty; but, as Milgram reminds us, ordinary Americans performed a variety of inhumane actions during the Vietnam War, including the massacre of hundreds of unarmed civilian men, women, and children. Milgram postulates that man's capacity to lose his humanity when subordinating his individuality to an institutional structure actually threatens the survival of our species.

This is a fatal flaw nature has designed into us, and which in the long run gives our species only a modest chance of survival.

It is ironic that the virtues of loyalty, discipline and self-sacrifice that we value so highly in the individual are the very properties that create destructive organizational engines of war and bind men to malevolent systems of authority.[11]

A third factor which facilitates violent and cruel behavior by normal people is the interposition of distance between perpetrator and victim. In this context, distance can be either physical or psychological. It is usually a mixture of both. If all human disputes were confined to fistfights, there would not only be fewer deaths but fewer instances of cruelty. Konrad Lorenz has argued that inhibitory mechanisms against injuring and killing one's own kind are poorly developed in human beings and easily overcome because man is not armed with dangerous natural weapons like tusks and claws. "A lion or a wolf may, on extremely rare occasions, kill another by one angry stroke, but . . . all heavily armed carnivores possess sufficiently reliable inhibitions which prevent the self-destruction of the species."[12]

As noted in the first chapter, the invention of weapons which kill at a distance has overridden any lingering inhibitions against killing other human beings. It has also facilitated the commission of acts of cruelty. A pilot who drops napalm upon people he cannot see may do so with no feeling of guilt. If he were ordered to pour gasoline over a child and then ignite it, he might well recoil and disobey. Yet the injuries inflicted would be closely similar. As Lorenz has argued:

> The deep, emotional layers of our personality simply do not register the fact that the crooking of the fore-finger to release a shot tears the entrails of another man. No sane man would even go rabbit-hunting for pleasure if the necessity of killing his prey with his natural weapons brought home to him the full emotional realization of what he is actually doing.[13]

In light of what happened in the Nazi concentration camps, this view of human nature may seem too idealistic; but the point about physical distance is still worth making. As we know from the examples of Hiroshima and Nagasaki, the destruction nuclear weapons can bring about is almost unimaginably vast. Yet human beings can be found who state that they would not hesitate to destroy whole cities and kill or maim thousands of human beings by dispatching an intercontinental ballistic missile if ordered to do so. As we remarked in chapter 2, disasters which take place in remote countries do not touch our hearts.

Psychological distance is an equally important factor contributing to man's destructiveness. By psychological distance I mean the capacity to treat other human beings as inferior, alien, or in extreme cases, less than human. We are all prone to attach stereotypes to social groups which differ from our own. In Britain, the Scots used to be labeled stingy, the Welsh dishonest, and the Irish feckless and alcoholic. Research has shown that some stereotypes are relatively persistent, whilst others change with changes in political and social relationships. Princeton students were asked to select from a very long list typical traits describing various ethnic groups. In 1951, not so long after Pearl Harbor, the Japanese were labeled "imitative, sly, extremely nationalistic, treacherous." In 1967, the list read "industrious, ambitious, efficient, intelligent, progressive." In 1951, Negroes were characterized as "superstitious, musical, lazy, ignorant, pleasure-loving." In 1967, the list had changed to "musical, happy-go-lucky, lazy, pleasure-loving, ostentatious."[14] Although the Negro stereotype is hardly complimentary, it is not as pejorative as the stereotype of a national group almost totally unknown to Princeton students: "Turks were characterized by three generations of Princetonians as *cruel, treacherous, sensual, ignorant,* and *dirty,* but hardly a single Princetonian had ever met a real-life Turk."[15] This is an instance of psychological distance facilitating the attribution of undesirable characteristics. The less we actually know or mix with a particular group of people, the easier it is to suppose them evil.

The tendency to form hierarchies, which we share with other social animals, ensures that all human societies are stratified to some extent. As Orwell put it, "All animals are equal but some animals are more equal than others."[16] All human beings are deeply preoccupied with status. Ethnocentrism, the belief in the superiority of one's own cultural group or society combined with derogation of other groups, is found throughout the world.

> It is not just the seeming universality of ethnocentrism that makes us think it ineradicable but rather that it has been traced to its source in individual psychology, and the source is the individual effort to achieve and maintain positive self-esteem. That is an urge so deeply human that we can hardly imagine its absence.[17]

It has often been remarked that strikes ostensibly concerned with obtaining higher pay often have much more to do with status than with money; that is, with preserving an undermined or threatened position in the hierarchy of the social structure. The creation or preservation of an underclass of slaves, servants, or laborers is particularly welcome to those in the grades immediately above it because it provides a social group to whom they can feel superior.

In the southern states of the U.S., various traditions have contributed to stereotypes of the black population which led to lynchings and other types of extremely cruel behavior in the not so distant past. The desire to maintain white supremacy is an obvious motive; but it is noteworthy that most lynchings occurred in poor rural counties where blacks were greatly outnumbered by whites. In counties where the white population was dependent upon blacks for labor, lynchings were far fewer. In counties where the black population was in economic competition with the white population, lynchings were more common. "It was the poor whites who were the usual lynchers."[18] Since poor whites were near the bottom of the heap, and therefore lacking in self-esteem, they had a particular need of a still lower grade to which they could feel superior, and which they often treated with contempt and cruelty.

In addition, blacks have often been considered a sexual threat. I have myself been in a hospital ward full of soldiers who alleged that once a white woman had known a black man sexually, she would never again be satisfied with a white lover. "You see, they're bigger made than we are." This unsupported belief underlies some of the fear and hatred directed toward black males in the South and also accounts for the fact that many lynchings included castration of the victim.

The various stereotypes mentioned above may not

all strike the reader as crazy. Blacks may or may not be particularly potent sexually; Turks may or may not be cruel; Irishmen may or may not be prone to alcoholism. Such widely held beliefs are generalizations which are not substantiated by much evidence but are not totally irrational. However, many societies have gone further in the direction of irrationality by creating pariah groups which act as scapegoats for the majority society. Beliefs about pariah groups hover on the brink of being delusional.

Stratification manifests itself in two main systems, class and caste. Class is the less rigid of the two, since mobility between classes is permissible though sometimes difficult to achieve. Membership in a class as a particular group within a culture is principally determined by the display of characteristics belonging to that class: by accent, interests, life-style, education, and so on, rather than by birth or place of origin. It is only loosely related to income and occupation, although these are the referents used in statistical definitions of social class. Class tends to be perpetuated by intermarriage, but there are no rules forbidding marriage between individuals from different classes, which are not infrequent. Hence, the distinctions between classes are often blurred.

In contrast, caste is much more rigid. Caste membership is determined by birth and remains constant throughout life. Endogamy is strictly enforced. Caste is closely allied with occupation, and some occupations, such as those involving the carcasses of dead animals, are felt to be intrinsically polluting. Butchers, tanners, and leatherworkers have been regarded as unclean in both India and Japan. In India, the caste system originally defined five grades: priests, princes, merchants, ordinary people, and polluted people. The virtuous individual accepted his station in life and acquired merit by performing the tasks appropriate to it. Rewards for virtue were granted in the next life rather than in the present one. The caste system is usually deplored by Western observers, but it made a positive contribution to social stability. Gandhi shocked many Indians by admitting an untouchable family to his ashram; but he opposed only those aspects of the caste system which were manifestly unjust, as the following quotation from his own writings demonstrates.

> From the economic point of view, its value was once very great. It ensured hereditary skill; it limited competition. It was the best remedy against pauperism. . . . Historically speaking, caste may be regarded as man's experiment on social adjustment in the laboratory of Indian society. If it can prove to be a success it can be offered to the world as a leaven and as the best remedy against heartless competition and social disintegration born of avarice and greed.[19]

Indian concepts of purity and pollution appear to stem from concerns about eating and excretion which every culture exhibits in varying degree, and which may originally have been derived from rational considerations of hygiene and disease prevention. Such concerns easily become emotionally exaggerated, as we know from the study of obsessional neurotics, who feel compelled to perform elaborate rituals in order to protect themselves against contamination. Compulsive hand-washing is only one of many varieties of such rituals. Creating a special caste of untouchables supposedly assigned by Nature or God to perform society's dirty work is thought to preserve and enhance the purity of the dominant groups.

In Japan, the creation of a pariah group outside society went further. The Burakumin, or "people of special communities," are descendants of a pariah caste still discriminated against both socially and economically. Originally, there were two groups: itinerant entertainers, fortune-tellers, and prostitutes; and tanners, leatherworkers, and animal slaughterers, comparable with the group discriminated against in India. The Burakumin can be distinguished from the Japanese majority only by records of their birthplace and residence, not by any physical characteristics. Nevertheless, they are considered "mentally inferior, incapable of high moral behaviour, aggressive, impulsive, and lacking any notion of sanitation or manners. Very often, they are 'the last hired and the first fired.' "[20] Various pejorative epithets have been applied to the Burakumin, such as *eta*, meaning "filth-abundant," or *yotsu*, meaning "four-legged." Their ancestors were designated "nonhuman." In this context, it is revealing to learn that the Japanese word for "lowly" (*iyashii*) is derived from a word meaning "mysterious and suspicious" (*ayashii*).[21] It is characteristic that pariah castes are not only despised as dirty and inferior but feared because they are thought to possess magical powers they may use to harm the "legitimate" society. It is when a particular section of a community is regarded as both *dangerous* and *despicable* that we are likely to encounter the extremes of human cruelty.

Since this chapter is predominantly concerned with giving some account of the propensity for cruelty in ordinary people, it may seem odd to title it "The Ubiquity of Paranoia"; for the noun "paranoia" and its corresponding adjective "paranoid" conjure up some of the most severe forms of mental illness. However, it is my belief that the psychological mechanisms which give rise to paranoid delusions in the psychotic can also be seen to operate in normal people; and that under certain circumstances, all of us are liable to entertain beliefs about other people which can only be labeled paranoid and may lead us to behave badly to those people.

If I were to ask any of my psychiatric colleagues to explain what they mean by the word "paranoid," they would begin by referring to the mechanism of *projection*, which may be defined as the process of attributing to others characteristics actually belonging to oneself. In the majority of cases, projection is a defense mechanism. The individual who cannot accept unpleasant aspects of his own nature, such as lust or greed, denies their existence in himself but is particularly prone to detect them in others. When someone vehemently accuses the gay community of corrupting youth and destroying the fabric of society, we can be fairly sure that he has never come to terms with his own homosexual impulses.

120

However, projection is not confined to negative feelings. Idealization is also a form of projection. We expect that a man in love will perceive his beloved as the acme of perfection and be temporarily blind to her failings. He is projecting upon her an idealized image of woman which originates within himself and will inevitably be modified in the course of time if he gets to know her better.

Positive images are projected upon authorities of all types, from political leaders and generals to clergymen and physicians. Freud's analysis of transference shows that analysands invariably project upon the analyst qualities derived from internalized images of their own parents. I have encountered paranoid patients who were convinced that behind their backs I was engaged in complicated negotiations and conspiracies to benefit them.

Sometimes patients project alternating images upon the analyst, treating him as if he were God on Tuesday and the Devil on Wednesday. Although I am not a Kleinian, I recognize that Melanie Klein's delineation of the so-called *paranoid-schizoid position* is a valuable insight. Klein postulated that at the beginning of life, the infant's first "object," the mother's breast, splits into two objects, one "good" because gratifying, and the other "bad" because frustrating. It is only later in development, with the attainment of what Klein calls the *depressive position*, that the infant becomes capable of recognizing that the same object can be frustrating at one time, gratifying at another.

Whatever the origin of this split into wholly good

121

and wholly bad, I am convinced that there is a level of mind, operative in all of us, at which images of the wholly good and the wholly bad persist. These images are particularly likely to be resuscitated in times of crisis, whether the crisis is personal or involves a whole group or country. When threatened, we look for saviors and devils: saviors who will rescue us, devils to blame for our predicament. Whether the images projected are positive or negative, their common feature is that the subject attributes to selected people great, often magical powers of good and evil whilst regarding himself as comparatively weak and helpless. In crises, a minority are prepared to lead; the majority regress to a state reminiscent of childhood, thankful to be told what to do. None of us are immune from according our leaders misplaced veneration, particularly in times of disaster or political upheaval. If the authority turns out to be malignant, like Hitler, veneration may blind his disciples to his true nature, and this, combined with obedience, can become a recipe for cruelty.

The victim of a fully developed paranoid psychosis commonly exhibits delusions of persecution. He believes that he is the center of hostile attention from enemies, who may be thought to belong to a particular group in society, perhaps Freemasons, Roman Catholics, or Jews. These wicked persons torment him in various subtle, complex ways. For instance, they may pump poison gases into his room at night or use electrical machines to cause him bizarre physical sensations. Today, when bombs can be exploded by remote control, he will affirm that there is nothing odd about supposing

122

that electronic devices can be used to torment people at a distance.

Even his thoughts are not his own. His enemies have ways of inserting alien thoughts into his mind, obscene sexual fantasies which would never ordinarily have occurred to him. Moreover, they have ways of broadcasting these thoughts so that other people have access to what he had supposed was intimate and private. This, no doubt, is why so many people look at him strangely when he goes out into the street, often muttering to each other that there is something peculiar about him. He has even heard voices accusing him of being homosexual or sexually perverted in some way.

He cannot entirely explain why he should be the center of so much attention. It has occurred to him that he may really be of royal descent rather than the son of his humble parents. At one time he was sure that he was in touch with the inhabitants of some other planet, who were giving him important instructions about saving the world from nuclear disaster. Perhaps his enemies are really armaments dealers who have a vested interest in ensuring that every nation is supplied with nuclear weapons . . .

The paranoid psychotic is expressing a split not only between good and evil, between his spotless self and his malignant persecutors, but also between helplessness and omnipotence. He is powerless against the evil forces trying to destroy him; but at the same time, he is clearly a person of importance, since so many people are concerned to persecute him.

It is hard to escape the conclusion that paranoia

represents a persistence into adult life of some aspects of infantile experience. Human babies are helpless in that they are dependent upon adults for their survival for several years after birth. Yet because of their helplessness, they are also the center of the household, and thus of signal importance. The distressing cases of child abuse discussed at the beginning of this chapter demonstrate that because of this centrality babies threaten the self-esteem of insecure men who feel themselves supplanted. It is not surprising that omnipotence and helplessness march hand in hand in cases of paranoid schizophrenia. Traces of the same phenomenon can be detected in all of us.

We may imagine that so-called normal people could never believe in anything so ludicrous as the delusional systems of the insane. Yet historical evidence suggests the opposite. Whole societies have been persuaded without much difficulty to accept the most absurd calumnies about minority groups portrayed as enemies of the majority. Such accusations originate from a particular type of fantasy which is comparable with, indeed equivalent to, paranoid delusions of the kind found in psychotic subjects.

> The essence of the fantasy was that there existed, somewhere in the midst of the great society, another society, small and clandestine, which not only threatened the existence of the great society but was also addicted to practices which were felt to be wholly abominable, in the literal sense of anti-human.[22]

The practices of which this clandestine society was accused included ritual slaughter of babies or young children, often accompanied by drinking their blood; cannibal feasts at which their remains were eaten; erotic orgies featuring every variety of sexual behavior, including homosexuality and incest; and a caricature of religion, either in the form of paying homage to the genitals of the presiding "priest" or else in worshiping an animal, frequently a donkey.

In other words, the clandestine society was regarded as a pariah group deliberately transgressing most of the basic rules which regulate human behavior. All known societies have taboos against incest, and many prohibit or disapprove of homosexuality and bestiality. Children are generally supposed to be cherished and protected, except in special circumstances. Cannibalism is usually confined to ritual eating of enemies after victories or successful raids. Conformity to the religion of the majority is encouraged, even if not enforced. The fantasied practices of the clandestine society sound like a list of all the worst sins the conformist citizen can think of, and so combine to constitute an image of absolute evil which, as I suggested above, may be a relic of the paranoid-schizoid stage of emotional development. The projection of such an image upon a minority group makes that group appear even more repulsive and dangerous than a pariah caste.

The above accusations were leveled at small, scattered groups of Christians in the Roman Empire during the second century after Christ, and they contributed to the savagery of the recurrent persecutions. Christians were also held responsible for natural disasters, such as floods, famines, plagues, and earthquakes. Persecuting the Christians as scapegoats no doubt distracted the general public from dwelling too closely upon the social dislocation a natural disaster might bring in its train. Nothing unites a divided society so effectively as identifying a common enemy. Citizens who might otherwise be at each other's throats will close ranks if propaganda has persuaded them that they face a shared threat.

At a later period in history, the Christians themselves made very similar accusations about witches. For centuries, elderly widows and spinsters were singled out by villagers who needed scapegoats to blame for natural misfortunes. Although in theory men or even children could be witches, it was principally old women who were thought to possess special powers to harm their neighbors (*maleficium*). In the late Middle Ages these alleged powers were made more fearsome and more culpable by being linked with heresy. It was widely believed that bereaved, neglected, or poverty-stricken women entered into pacts with the Devil, who conferred certain malignant powers upon them in return for their allegiance: occult powers enabling them to damage crops, to bring about illness in beasts and human beings, to kill small children, and to interfere with sexual relationships by causing abortion or sterility in women and impotence in men. Witches were said to manufacture from the flesh of slaughtered infants an ointment which enabled them to fly when applied to their bodies. On three or four occasions throughout the year, witches were supposed to attend a gathering called a *sabbat*. The Devil presided at such meetings and conducted a service which was a parody of the Christian Eucharist. An erotic orgy followed, in which the Devil copulated with each participant.

*Malleus Maleficarum*, "the Hammer of Witches," is a treatise for witch-hunters which first appeared in 1486. It was written by two inquisitors of the Catholic church, Heinrich Kramer and James Sprenger, who were specially appointed by Pope Innocent VIII to root out witchcraft throughout northern Germany. The book contains detailed instructions about recognizing witches, proceeding against them judicially, torturing them, and pronouncing sentence upon them. By modern standards, it is a horrifying manual of psychopathology which demonstrates how easily men can build up delusional systems about the power of women.

> It must be said, as was shown in the preceding inquiry, that three general vices appear to have special dominion over wicked women, namely, infidelity, ambition, and lust. Therefore they are more than others inclined toward witchcraft, who more than others are given to these vices. Again, since of these three vices the last chiefly predominates, women being insatiable etc., it follows that those among ambitious women are more deeply infected who are more hot to satisfy their filthy lusts; and such are adulteresses, fornicatresses, and the concubines of the Great.
>
> Now there are, as it is said in the Papal Bull, seven methods by which they infect with witchcraft the venereal act and the conception of the womb. First, by inclin-

ing the minds of men to inordinate passion; second, by obstructing their generative force; third, by removing the members accommodated to that act; fourth, by changing men into beasts by their magic art; fifth, by destroying the generative force in women; sixth, by procuring abortion; seventh, by offering children to devils, besides other animals and fruits of the earth with which they work much harm.[23]

A long section discusses "diabolic operations with regard to the male organ," asking "whether witches can with the help of devils really and actually remove the member or whether they only do so apparently by some glamour or illusion."[24] Such questions may amuse us until we recall the persecution and torture of innocent women which they prompted.

We may think that the credulity of the Middle Ages has no parallel in our own day, but the Reverend Montague Summers, English editor and translator of *Malleus Maleficarum*, and author of *The History of Witchcraft and Demonology* and *The Geography of Witchcraft*, believed wholeheartedly in what he was writing about. *Malleus Maleficarum* is a monstrous, horrifying farrago of paranoid delusions, but Summers alleges that it contains "seemingly inexhaustible wells of wisdom." He goes on:

What is most surprising is the modernity of the book. There is hardly a problem, a complex, a difficulty, which they have not foreseen, and discussed, and resolved.

Here are cases which occur in the law-courts today,

> set out with the greatest clarity, argued with unflinching
> logic, and judged with scrupulous impartiality. . . . The
> *Malleus Maleficarum* is one of the world's few books
> written *sub specie aeternitatis.*[25]

The introduction from which this quotation is taken is
dated October 7, 1946!

The idea that old women could wreak harm upon
their neighbors by magical means was current for many
centuries. Although accurate figures are hard to come
by, there is no doubt that many hundreds of innocent
women were accused, tortured, and burned. But the
"great witch-hunt," in which a million may have perished, occupied a relatively short period of about a
century.

> It reached its height only in the late sixteenth century,
> and it was practically over by 1680—with the trials at
> Salem, Massachusetts, in 1692 as a belated epilogue. It
> was an exclusively western phenomenon—eastern Eu-
> rope, the world of Orthodox Christianity, was un-
> touched by it.[26]

The historian Norman Cohn concludes that what had
been the persecution of eccentric individuals turned into
a mass witch-hunt because witches came to be regarded
as a heretical sect meeting to plot the overthrow of
Christianity and orthodox society. In other words,
witches were seen as a conspiratorial, clandestine out-
group comparable to the Christian out-groups per-
secuted during the second century. The Christians were

accused of posing a threat to Greco-Roman orthodoxy; witches were said to constitute a threat to Christianity, and their *sabbats* were supposed to involve ritual practices which infringed or inverted the basic laws governing Christian behavior.

The slaughter of five to six million Jews in the concentration camps of Nazi Germany was discussed earlier in connection with the part played by obedience to authority in the commission of acts of cruelty. Amongst many other factors, two require further comment in this context. The first is the underlying persistence of a fantasy about Jews which, like beliefs about witches, has its roots in the Middle Ages. The second is the deliberate degradation of the victims to make them appear repulsive and subhuman, with the result that ordinary people could more easily participate in abusing and killing them. As noted above, it is when a particular group of human beings is regarded as both dangerous and despicable that we encounter the extremes of human cruelty.

Paranoid fantasies about Jews, like those about Christians, can be traced back as far as the second century A.D., when leaders of the Christian church wanted to encourage their followers to make a final break with Judaism. To this end, they began to refer to Jews as habitual murderers, sons of Satan, and followers of the Antichrist. By the twelfth century, the myth had been elaborated in such a way as to share many features already outlined above. Jews were accused of ritually murdering Christian children, of torturing the consecrated wafer, of poisoning wells, and of worshiping the

Devil. It was widely believed that the blood of Christian children was used to make unleavened bread for Passover. Jews were accused of practicing black magic and conspiring to destroy Christendom. Although in reality Jews were broadly dispersed and not subject to any centralized Jewish authority, a widespread belief held that there was a council of rabbis based in Spain which constituted a secret government directing operations against Christians. Thus Jews, like witches, came to be regarded as a conspiratorial, clandestine out-group dedicated to the overthrow of the majority society.

In his seminal book *Warrant for Genocide*, Norman Cohn has demonstrated that medieval paranoid fantasies about a Jewish conspiracy were revived in modern dress and provided at least part of the motive force behind the Holocaust.

> Exterminatory antisemitism appears where Jews are imagined as a collective embodiment of evil, a conspiratorial body dedicated to ruining and then dominating the rest of mankind. This kind of antisemitism can exist almost regardless of the real situation of Jews in society. It can prosper where Jews form a large, cohesive and clearly recognizable minority, but also where the only Jews are a few scattered individuals who hardly regard themselves as Jews at all. And if it thrives in the spectacle of rich and influential Jews, it does not necessarily wilt where all Jews are poor. Most striking of all, it can be found among people who have never set eyes on a Jew and in countries where there have been no Jews for centuries.[27]

131

The vehicle which disseminated the myth of a Jewish world conspiracy in modern times was a malicious forgery known as *The Protocols of the Elders of Zion*. This enormously influential book, which attained world-wide circulation during the 1920s and 1930s, purported to be lecture notes in which a member of the secret Jewish central government, the Elders of Zion, reveals the Jewish plot to achieve world domination. In briefest outline, the idea is that by fomenting unrest and revolution, combined with sly financial manipulation, the Jews will finally gain supreme power and set up a world state, politically controlled by a vast army of secret police and ruled by a Jewish sovereign of the House of David.

This ludicrous fantasy became a keystone of Nazi propaganda and was extensively employed by Rosenberg, Streicher, and Goebbels to foment anti-Semitism. *The Protocols* was even prescribed as a school textbook shortly after Hitler came to power. There is no doubt that many influential people, including the commandant of Auschwitz, regarded the extermination of European Jewry as necessary to counter the threat of world domination. Even so sober a journal as the London *Times* devoted an article to *The Protocols* on May 8, 1920.

> Are they a forgery? If so, whence comes the uncanny note of prophecy, prophecy in parts fulfilled, in parts far gone in the way of fulfilment? Have we been struggling these tragic years to blow up and extirpate the secret organization of German world dominion only to find beneath it another, more dangerous because more se-

cret? Have we, by straining every fibre of our national body, escaped a "Pax Germanica" only to fall into a "Pax Judaeica"? The "Elders of Zion" as represented in their "Protocols" are by no means kinder taskmasters than William II and his henchmen would have been.[28]

*The Spectator* went further. On October 16, 1920, it published an editorial suggesting the establishment of a commission to investigate whether or not there was a worldwide Jewish conspiracy to destroy Christianity. *Blackwood's Magazine* demanded that Jews be excluded from all positions of influence. The conspiracy theory was still current in Britain in 1935. Major General J. F. C. Fuller, a distinguished soldier and tank expert and a convert to fascism, wrote an article entitled "The Cancer of Europe" in which he stated:

> The predominant characteristic of the Jew is his materialism which endows him with a destructive social force when he is placed in a spiritually ordered society. . . . By predilection a trader, a banker, a dabbler in the occult, like a mole he works underground, silently and hidden, and like a bat he flits through the night seeing things unseen by creatures of day. . . . Self-defence has compelled him to rely upon craft and cunning, always the weapons of the weak, and to enter into alliance with every subversive movement. In these Jews see power—power to avenge their wrongs, and power to gain world domination under an avenging messiah—as foretold by Talmud and Qabalah.[29]

This brief quotation contains all the hallmarks of paranoid projection. A rejected out-group, weak though it may appear on the surface, has secret occult powers which it is intent on using against the majority society. It is despicable and dangerous simultaneously.

When Hitler came to power, he exploited the paranoid potential latent in the minds of men more successfully than any other leader has ever done. He was building on a long tradition of quasireligious mystical writings claiming that there had once been a golden age in which an uncorrupted race of Aryans had ruled supreme. Nicholas Goodricke-Clarke has recorded the extraordinary but influential racist and nationalist fantasies of writers like Guido von List and Lanz von Liebenfels. If anyone still questions the power which myth, as opposed to reason, exercises over the human mind, he should read *The Occult Roots of Nazism*: "Semi-religious beliefs in a race of Aryan god-men, the needful extermination of inferiors, and a wonderful millennial future of German world-domination obsessed Hitler, Himmler, and many other high-ranking Nazi leaders."[30] The Aryans, blue-eyed, blond-haired, noble, courageous, were the original German race which had been undermined by intermarriage with inferior breeds, but under Hitler's guidance, they could once again establish their natural superiority as leaders of mankind. The Aryans of course represented the "wholly good" side of the paranoid equation. Ranged against them was a variety of enemies, including socialists, Bolsheviks, and Freemasons; but all these criminals were actually controlled by the Jews, who thus represented the "wholly bad" side of the paranoid equation.

The demoralization of Germany after its defeat in the First World War was intensified by the punitive terms of the Versailles treaty and the collapse of the currency in 1923. When Hitler first attempted to seize power, in November 1923, it took four billion marks to buy a dollar. The "Beer Hall Putsch" was a failure; but after serving a prison sentence during which he dictated *Mein Kampf*, Hitler bided his time until another opportunity offered itself. Between 1925 and 1929 economic and social conditions improved, but the U.S. stock market crash of October 1929 heralded the onset of a widespread economic depression which closed many businesses and threw millions of Germans out of work. The more insecure and helpless people feel, the more will they look for a savior to rescue them and a scapegoat to blame for the crisis. The pattern of social collapse followed by the emergence of a leader who both makes promises of a millennium to come and identifies the enemies of the society is a familiar one which has repeated itself throughout history.

> The appeal of Nazism was based on powerful fantasies designed to relieve acute feelings of anxiety, defeat, and demoralization. An anti-German conspiracy of Jews and their minions was supposed to be threatening the very survival of the German nation. The Socialists, the "November criminals" (the signatories of the shameful 1918 armistice), the Bolsheviks, the Freemasons, and even modern artists were all seen as agents of a monstrous Jewish plot to destroy Germany. Only the total destruction of the Jews could thus save the Germans and enable them to enter the promised land.[31]

In addition, Jews were held responsible for the white slave traffic, prostitution, and the spread of syphilis. A Jew who had sexual relations with a Christian girl was accused of adulterating her blood. Every evil in society was blamed on the Jews.

Such considerations go some way toward explaining the systematic extermination of five to six million Jews in the concentration camps. Although helpless in the hands of their persecutors, the Jews were still credited with possessing malignant powers, still felt as a potential threat to the German state.

In addition, measures were adopted in the camps to break the prisoners as individuals and make them appear subhuman. The more human beings are perceived as alien, the easier it becomes to inflict violence upon them or to slaughter them. The potentially inhibitory effect of helplessness is easily overridden if the victim is regarded as subhuman. Prisoners in the concentration camps were inadequately clothed, malnourished, and forced to perform hard labor. It was impossible to stay clean, and many prisoners soon lost any concern with personal hygiene. Dysentery was rife, toilet facilities were grossly inadequate, and permission to use latrines during the working day was often refused. Prisoners were frequently covered with their own excrement and smelled repulsive as well as looking like filthy scarecrows. The commandant of Treblinka, Franz Stangl, was asked why such humiliation was employed since the prisoners were going to be killed in any case. He replied, "To condition those who actually had to carry out the policies. To make it possible for them to do what they did.''[32]

Cruelty and destructiveness of this order is peculiar to the human species because it requires the operation of the imagination. It represents the nether side of man's most priceless asset. To be able to see fellow human beings as wholly evil, as possessing magical powers for harm, as being both despicable and dangerous, requires an imaginative capacity not found in other species. In another book, I have argued that man's capacity for imagination is biologically adaptive.[33] Our superiority to other animals and our partial mastery of the environment depend upon an innate discontent with what is, which compels a resort to imagination to invent something better. And imagination knows no limits. Man's greatest achievements, both in the arts and in the sciences, depend upon his imagination.

But what can be used for good can also be used for evil. Goya, without doubt the greatest painter of horror, knew what he was writing about when he prefaced *Los Caprichos* with the famous sentence ''Fantasy abandoned by reason produces impossible monsters; united with her, she is the mother of the arts and the origin of their marvels.''[34] Men are irresistibly attracted by fantasies in which reason is abandoned. In an impossibly complex universe, we long for simplicity, for a world divided into black and white. The appeal of a great deal of imaginative fiction depends upon this vision, from Tolkien's *Lord of the Rings* to science-fiction comics. Apocalyptic fantasies, disguised, refined, dressed up in

all kinds of ways, are the foundation of most fiction
concerned with heroes and villains, and of much else as
well. Even the sober-minded Freud concluded that life
is a struggle between Eros and Death which he called a
"battle of the giants."

When men divide the world into good and evil,
into sheep and goats, what happens to the goats is usually horrible.

> And I saw a new heaven and a new earth: for the first
> heaven and the first earth were passed away; and there
> was no more sea.
>
> And I John saw the holy city, new Jerusalem, com-
> ing down from God out of heaven, prepared as a bride
> adorned for her husband.
>
> And I heard a great voice out of heaven saying,
> Behold, the tabernacle of God is with men, and he will
> dwell with them, and they shall be his people, and God
> himself shall be with them, and be their God.
>
> And God shall wipe away all tears from their eyes;
> and there shall be no more death, neither sorrow nor
> crying, neither shall there be any more pain; for the
> former things are passed away.[35]

But John's millenniary vision of total harmony and
goodness was of course preceded by a vision of the Last
Judgment. Gassing by Zyklon-B was beyond the reach
of John's imagination, but being cast into a lake of fire is
only marginally less ghastly.

> And I saw the dead, small and great, stand before God;
> and the books were opened: and another book was

opened which is the book of life: and the dead were judged out of those things which were written in the books, according to their works.

And the sea gave up the dead which were in it; and death and hell delivered up the dead which were in them: and they were judged every man according to their works.

And death and hell were cast into the lake of fire. This is the second death.

And whosoever was not found written in the book of life was cast into the lake of fire.[36]

# 5

---

## *"What Is to Be Done?"*

My CHOICE of heading for this last chapter is of course ironic. Chernyshevsky's famous novel *What Is to Be Done?* is described as "a social Utopia which, grotesque as a work of art, had a literally epoch-making effect on Russian opinion" before the Revolution.[1] It was greatly admired by Lenin, who wrote an equally famous essay of the same title. As may be surmised from the previous chapter, my own views are profoundly anti-Utopian. I think that *Homo sapiens* has not altered very much in fundamental physical or psychological characteristics since he first appeared upon the scene; and that the best we can hope for is some slight modification of his nastier traits of personality in light of increased understanding. We cannot abolish man's potential for cruelty and destructiveness, but we may be partially able to control the circumstances which lead to their overt expression.

I do not share Melanie Klein's hope that her variety of analysis will become a part of every child's upbringing and that man's hostility will be diminished as a consequence. I do not believe that there is any one political system, religious faith, psychoanalytic school, scientific attitude, or philosophical point of view which has sole access to the truth. My dogma is that all dogma is suspect; and it seems to me that most of the harm in the world is done by those who are dogmatically certain that they are right. For being absolutely right means that those who disagree are absolutely wrong. Those who are absolutely wrong are of course dangerous to society and must be restrained or eliminated. That is the beginning of the road to the torture chamber and the gas oven.

This does not mean that I am without hope that human cruelty and destructiveness can be partly controlled and somewhat diminished. It only means that I have no single recipe, no overall plan, no blueprint, and no Utopian vision. I find myself in agreement with Karl Popper, whose plea is that we should never aim at revolution, only at piecemeal reform. Revolutions are one-sided affairs which are only too likely to result in a new regime as authoritarian and intolerant as the old regime it superseded. This was what happened after the

Russian Revolution of 1917. It is only when we are sufficiently mature to abandon the notion that there is any single solution to social problems, or any one person who is always right, that we can conduct the kind of critical debate which allows true progress to take place. The rest of this chapter is likely to be thought tautologous; but if it stimulates argument it will have served its purpose.

We live in a society in which ordinary people are increasingly alarmed by the threat of violence. Many will not venture out at night for fear that some thug will attack them. This is no new phenomenon; the streets of our big cities are probably safer today than they were in the eighteenth century. Even in the 1900s, parts of London were so violent that no policeman would venture in unaccompanied. From what has been said earlier, it is clear that violent crime will persist to some degree in any large society, since we cannot cure, eliminate, or prevent the birth of all individuals deemed to be suffering from aggressive personality disorders.

However, the evidence does suggest that by far the majority of violent offenses are committed by people from the lower levels of society, in which individuals are most likely to feel neglected, unappreciated, and of no account. Any measures which reduce inequality, alleviate poverty, and provide socially valued work, and which therefore raise self-esteem, are likely to reduce the level of violence. Severe punishments are largely ineffective, for reasons already detailed.

These statements are clichés; but one is compelled to reiterate them, since judges and governments still

143

seem to believe that lengthening prison sentences or bringing back corporal and capital punishment in countries which have abolished these penalties will prove a deterrent.

There is strong evidence suggesting that punitive methods of child-rearing are likely to produce aggressive children, for reasons outlined in chapter 2. We should therefore discourage such methods of child-rearing so far as we can. For example, we can actively oppose corporal punishment, both in schools and at home, in the confident expectation that its abandonment is likely to reduce rather than increase violent behavior.

There is also reason to believe that many habitually violent people have been unable to form close positive relationships with other human beings from childhood on. In some cases, failure of attachment can be traced to genetic defects, brain damage, or delay in maturation; in others, to inadequate, rejecting, or harshly punitive parents. It is platitudinous to affirm that children are more likely to develop into caring, affectionate adults who are not prone to violence if they have had caring, affectionate parents who not only proffer love but also provide positive models of identification. If all parents were of this kind, we can be fairly sure that violence would be less frequent; but we have no way of ensuring that parents behave decently.

Is there anything else which can sensibly be said about methods of child-rearing? The relation between early childhood experience and later behavior is far more complex and dubious than psychiatrists and educators used to believe. As Jerome Kagan has pointed out, the widespread assumption that the events of infancy are crucial for adult happiness is not securely based. Babies differ temperamentally, and "there probably is no best regimen for rearing all infants."[2] Kagan believes that some traits, like vulnerability to anxiety, can be detected as variables in infants from the very first days of life, long before attachment to a caretaker has had time to develop.

Moreover, varying assumptions are made about infants and their needs in different cultures and in different epochs. Freud's hypotheses about orality, Melanie Klein's theories of infantile aggression, and Piaget's ideas of cognitive development reflect cultural prejudices which are historically rather than observationally based. Americans see infants as wholly dependent and think of dependence as something which must be outgrown. Japanese see infants as possessing some degree of autonomy which must be tamed in order to ensure a cooperative adult.

Although Kagan is rightly skeptical about how far early experiences and childhood characteristics are preserved into adulthood, he does note that research has revealed that aggressive behavior in young boys is likely to persist. "The aggressive seven-year-old is likely to be an adolescent bully."[3] And he also admits:

> Even though we cannot measure with sensitivity the variations in the emotional quality of an infant's attachment, there is good reason for believing in the theoretical utility of this idea, for most infants living in

145

neglecting environments are more fearful, more labile, and less gleeful than those who have the benefit of predictable and loving care.[4]

In the first edition of this book, I made a plea for further research into different methods of rearing infants. I also quoted from my correspondence with Richard de Boer, an anthropologist who had made a special study of the Netsilik Eskimos. He claimed that cultures which employed the type of maternal infant caretaking known as "extero-gestation" produced adults from whom it was impossible or difficult to elicit interpersonal aggressive responses. Extero-gestation consists in trying to provide the newborn infant with an environment closely similar to the womb from which he has recently emerged.

> In these societies, infants are carried about constantly, slept with at night and the sensory route of communication is tactile which facilitates a response to infant stimuli (e.g. sucking and rooting reflex) that precludes crying behavior and restricts frustration to about the same level the infant enjoyed in utero where homeostasis is maintained biochemically through the mediatory functions of the placenta.[5]

This regime is maintained until the infant is independently mobile. De Boer claims that aggressive patterns are not innate but only become encoded in response to adverse external stimuli. In other words, he is propounding a version of the frustration-aggression hypothesis. If infants are never frustrated, they will not develop the cell structures and conditioned responses which underlie aggressive behavior in later life.

It is certainly true that Eskimo society was relatively peaceful until Western man interfered with it. When disputes arose between individuals, Eskimos dealt with them by ritualized song contests and drum duels. As described by Richard de Boer:

> The Eskimo culture is characterized by a social and economic anarchy. There are no leaders, chiefs or bosses and no Eskimo ever worked for another Eskimo, but many Eskimos often work together. Dominance hierarchies are not innate in species sapiens, dominance behavior is learned. . . . The Eskimo has practiced the precepts of Karl Marx for over five thousand years and during which time they maintained an unusually viable and stable culture without resorting to any kind of dominance hierarchy.[6]

Various anthropologists have affirmed that "natural" man is not competitive, hostile, possessive, or destructive; and accounts of a number of other preliterate societies echo de Boer's description of the Eskimos.

One characteristic shared by these societies is that they are extremely small. Another is that they are fast disappearing. We should also bear in mind that certain societies described by anthropologists in idyllic terms have later been shown to be far more aggressive than initial observations suggested. Nevertheless, it is important to keep an open mind about how far different

147

methods of child-rearing may influence later behavior, and we badly need more long-term follow-up studies. Anecdotally, I am impressed with the results of keeping small infants in very close contact with the mother for a considerable period after birth, and am in favor of feeding on demand and against leaving infants to cry for any prolonged period. It seems to me that children reared in this way are more equable, confident, and responsive; but this is merely an unsubstantiated opinion.

I suggested earlier that tripling the price of alcohol would reduce violence, and so it would. However, governments raise huge revenues from alcohol taxes and therefore have a vested interest in maintaining consumption. Moreover, alcohol in moderation is a valuable resource. As we know from past experience, prohibition not only does not work but has disastrous consequences in that it fosters organized crime and racketeering of every description. What to do about alcohol in relation to violent crime is a good example of an issue to which there are no clear-cut, easy solutions. It is exactly the kind of problem which cannot be solved by dictatorial decree but can be ameliorated by agreements reached after informed democratic discussion. The more recent escalation in drug use, which contributes so much to contemporary street violence, is a similar problem, but one requiring more specialist knowledge than I possess.

There can be no possible doubt that effective control of the sale of firearms, combined with stringent penalties for anyone possessing a firearm without a license, would reduce the incidence of homicide in those countries which do not impose such controls. Similar considerations apply to knives expressly designed for violence and to other weapons such as brass knuckles. Easy availability of lethal weapons increases the risk that otherwise transient quarrels will end in tragedy. This is so obvious as to constitute another cliché; but as we all know, some governments are very reluctant to introduce the necessary legal measures.

The question of censorship is still a vexed one. It seems generally agreed that there is little reason to suppose that reading materials directly cause violent behavior. In any case, many who commit violent offenses are virtually illiterate. We have already noted that the possession of pornography does not distinguish those who are likely to commit sexual offenses from those who are not. If we demanded thorough censorship of violent literature, we should have to prohibit the Bible for fear that someone might do what Jael did to Sisera or repeat the Crucifixion. Moreover, we should have to proscribe a large proportion of children's literature. Myths, legends, and fairy stories often contain scenes of an extremely violent kind. In the blinding of Polyphemus in the *Odyssey*, the giant's single eyeball crackles and hisses when the heated olive branch is plunged into it, and he is maddened with pain; yet no one seriously suggests that we should censor the *Odyssey*.

The effect of watching violent scenes in the cinema and on television is perhaps a different matter. According to some experimental psychologists, laboratory studies have demonstrated that aggressive acts can be evoked by the viewing of violent scenes, and that indi-

149

viduals may learn new forms of aggressive behavior from such viewing. Others dispute the validity of these studies, pointing out that laboratory investigations often seem remote from real life. When I served on the British Committee on Obscenity and Film Censorship (the Williams Committee), our review of the evidence led us to conclude that the influence of watching screen violence upon the commission of violent acts must be regarded as "not proven."

However, we saw a variety of films which contained explicit depictions of violent and cruel behavior of a revolting kind. Many of these films seemed to promulgate or reinforce the idea that inflicting pain and injury is pleasurable; and even those amongst us who, like myself, were initially and theoretically opposed to censorship agreed that some controls over such material ought to be exercised, because of its uncertain effect upon young people whose emotional development is incomplete. But censorship ought to be kept to a minimum. People whose tastes are established will always find a way around the censor; and the greater the censorship, the greater the underground criminal activity designed to satisfy those tastes. The idea that forbidding the portrayal of violence on television and in films, even if it were practicable, would have a profound effect in reducing the level of violence in society is almost certainly an illusion. The roots of violent behavior, as I hope I have indicated, lie deeper.

The role of obedience in relation to cruelty was explored in the last chapter. Can anything be done to diminish the human tendency to obey orders when those orders involve gross cruelty? Since obedience is biologically adaptive in social creatures, we cannot rid ourselves of the tendency to obey, even if we wished to do so. (I cannot agree with de Boer in supposing that all hierarchical behavior is learned rather than innate.) But I think the operation of this double-edged tendency could be modified. Today even military training is less insistent on immediate, unquestioning obedience than in former years. Modern ''conventional'' warfare favors operations carried out by small units, which have to be more autonomous than large armies and must be commanded by officers and noncommissioned officers who have the power to make independent decisions.

In addition, the Nuremberg trials of Nazi war criminals, and trials of soldiers who committed atrocities in Vietnam and elsewhere, have established that obedience is no longer considered a valid excuse for brutality. Since 1945, a detailed code of human rights has been elaborated in international law. Obedience to this code transcends obedience to commanding officers, prison authorities, government officials, and the like. Those who refuse to carry out torture, for example, may be risking their jobs, their freedom, or even their lives in certain countries, but all the international human rights instruments declare that ''no one shall be subjected to torture or to cruel, inhuman or degrading treatment or punishment.''

An American federal court has held that this prohibition has now become part of *customary* international law, so binding all nations and not only those that are parties to

151

the treaties. As that court put it: "The torturer has become—like the pirate and slave trader before him— *hostis humani generis*, an enemy of all mankind."[7]

Of course torture goes on; but the fact that there is an international code prohibiting it, and that torture is now regarded as a crime against humanity, will make it increasingly difficult for torturers to escape justice and will act as a partial deterrent.

Physicians are in a special position with regard to torture and may be able to play some part in preventing it. Physicians employed by prison and military services are often asked to examine prisoners prior to interrogations involving torture, and to evaluate their fitness to undergo further interrogation/torture. The purpose of such examinations is primarily to protect the torturer, who may want to avoid the consequences of causing a prisoner's death. The British Medical Association's *Handbook of Medical Ethics* unequivocally declares:

> It is unethical for a doctor to carry out an examination on a person before that person is interrogated under duress or tortured. Even though the doctor takes no part in the interrogation or torture, his examination of the patient prior to interrogation could be interpreted as condoning it.
>
> Whether or not a doctor should treat the effects of torture depends on whether the patient wants the doctor's help. The doctor himself must be prepared to use all his skills to help a patient, whatever the cause of the injuries. But if the victim of torture prefers to die, the doctor must respect the patient's wishes.[8]

Even in democratic countries, a great deal of cruelty goes on in prisons, partly because they are closed institutions to which the public has very little access, and are therefore difficult to monitor. During my training as a psychiatrist, I worked in two British prisons. I was required to sign the Official Secrets Act, which involved promising not to make public anything I learned as a result of my privileged access. This is an absurd requirement. Individual case histories of prisoners should not be revealed without their consent, but everything else which goes on in prisons should be public property. Secrecy and unnecessary concealment foster abuses, as we know from the interrogation methods employed in prisons in Northern Ireland. When these first came to light in the early 1970s, public opinion was shocked and a variety of inquiries were instituted. I have told the story elsewhere[9] and will therefore give only a brief résumé.

Men detained as suspected terrorists were deprived of sleep, given only minimum rations of bread and water, and made to stand spread-eagled against a wall for hours at a time. In addition, they were hooded so that they could see nothing, and subjected to continuous "white noise" so that they could hear nothing other than this noise. After some hours or days of this treatment, detainees started to experience a variety of psychiatric symptoms, including hallucinations, and some became convinced that they were going mad. Follow-up studies of those released showed that such symptoms of psychiatric disturbance as insomnia, irritability, and depression persisted for months after the ordeal. After numerous protests, the British prime minister, then Edward Heath, forbade any further use of these methods of interrogation. Ireland then brought a case against Britain before the European Commission of Human Rights, sitting at Strasbourg. The commissioners decided that the methods of interrogation employed amounted to torture; but the Court of Human Rights later decided that the suffering inflicted did not amount to torture, although it did represent an example of "inhuman and degrading treatment." The point of recalling this deplorable story is that the interrogations had been undertaken without any high-ranking army officers or policemen overseeing them or accepting responsibility. This kind of abuse can only take place behind closed doors. A good deal of cruelty could undoubtedly be prevented if prisons were more easily open to inspection.

In the last chapter, we saw that the interposition of physical distance between perpetrator and victim facilitates violent and cruel behavior. Not much can be done to circumvent this. We cannot disinvent weapons which kill at a distance, or insist that all fights be conducted face to face. But we can make sure that people actually understand what happens when a rifle bullet tears through a man's body, when a high-explosive bomb is dropped on a village, or when a nuclear weapon is dropped on a city. One of the objections to violence on television is that it is not violent enough. Although there have been protests at the amount of blood spilled in the films of Sam Peckinpah and others, it is still violence sanitized and made tolerable because we know it is faked. When a man is shot in the stomach, we do not see his guts hanging out. We do not see people in agony vomiting and losing control of their sphincters: "The media do not depict violence; they depict a bowdlerized version of violence. It is strange that when films do seek for reality, they have a high likelihood of being banned, but when they idealize violence the risk of such a consequence is slight."[10] I am not advocating that violence on television and in films should be made more horribly realistic than it is. But I think it important that there should be exhibitions and museums which preserve records and photographs of what actually happens in war, in concentration camps, and in other situations in which extreme violence is employed.

In the first chapter, I recalled that my own concern with problems of human destructiveness and violence was provoked by newsreel films of the concentration camps. Some people have considered it morbid of the Jews to ensure that these horrors are thoroughly documented and to insist that the public is constantly reminded of them. I do not agree. Men easily forget; and tend to forget unpleasant happenings more quickly than pleasant ones. It is vital that future generations understand the depths to which human nature can sink, vital that they realize that there is no limit to human cruelty and destructiveness, so that they will take what steps they can to see that such things are not repeated.

The same considerations apply to the use of nuclear

weapons. The bomb dropped on Hiroshima killed 140,000 people; the bomb dropped on Nagasaki killed 70,000. We are all familiar with the photographs of devastated Hiroshima and Nagasaki, but how many have really studied the injuries of the survivors, the death rate from nuclear-induced disease, and the genetic effects on future generations? We turn away from such dreadful things because we cannot bear too much reality.

Can anything be done to reduce or modify what I have called man's paranoid potential? In a world living under the perpetual threat of nuclear annihilation, it is particularly important that no one group or nation should perceive another as wholly evil and therefore seek its total destruction. Pessimists claim that mankind has learned nothing from history; but I believe that we are gradually learning more about the kind of crises and social conditions which provoke persecution and genocide. We cannot avoid natural catastrophes or social upheavals; but I think that in light of modern knowledge, Western nations may be less likely than formerly to create scapegoats and institute persecutions as a result of disasters or political changes. Historical education may not be able to achieve much, but it can achieve something. The Holocaust was so terrible that it may be less easy to blame the troubles of a nation upon a minority or out-group. Nuclear weapons are so terrible that they may have made it easier for us to avoid world war.

What chiefly concerns and alarms many of us are the problems arising from religious fanaticism. As long as large numbers of militant enthusiasts are persuaded that they alone have access to the truth, and that the rest of us are infidels, we remain under threat. Lord Acton's famous phrase about power can be used of another danger. Dogma tends to corrupt, and absolute dogma corrupts absolutely.

# Notes

## 1. *The Nature of Human Aggression*

1. Gerda Siann, *Accounting for Aggression* (London: Allen & Unwin, 1985), p. 227.

2. Ibid.

3. *The Marriage of Heaven and Hell: Poetry and Prose of William Blake* (London: Nonesuch Press, 1927), p. 201.

4. R. L. Trivers, quoted in Edward O. Wilson, *Sociobiology* (Cambridge, Mass.: Harvard University Press, 1975), pp. 341–42.

5. Siann, p. 241.

6. Tony Parker and Robert Allerton, *The Courage of His Convictions* (London: Hutchinson, 1962), p. 93.

7. Charles Rycroft, *A Critical Dictionary of Psychoanalysis* (New York: Basic Books, 1969), p. 5.

8. Nicholas Mosley, *Julian Grenfell* (London: Weidenfeld & Nicolson, 1976), pp. 238–39.

9. Charles Rycroft, "Introduction: Causes and Meaning," in Rycroft, ed., *Psychoanalysis Observed* (New York: Coward McCann, 1967), p. 21.

10. Paul Schilder, "Action, Impulsion, Aggression," in *Contributions to Developmental Neuro-Psychiatry* (New York: International Universities Press, 1964), p. 283.

11. D. W. Winnicott, "Aggression in Relation to Emotional Development," in M. Masuds and R. Khan, eds., *Through Paediatrics to Psycho-Analysis* (London: Hogarth Press, 1975), p. 204.

12. Clara M. Thompson, *Interpersonal Psycho-Analysis* (New York: Basic Books, 1964), p. 179.

13. Schilder, pp. 242–43.

14. Sigmund Freud, *Instincts and Their Vicissitudes*, Standard Edition, vol. 14 (London: Hogarth Press, 1957), p. 139.

15. Sigmund Freud, *Beyond the Pleasure Principle*, Standard Edition, vol. 18 (London: Hogarth Press, 1955), p. 36.

16. Ibid., p. 38.

17. Sigmund Freud, *Civilization and Its Discontents*, Standard Edition, vol. 21 (London: Hogarth Press, 1961), p. 121.

18. Winnicott, p. 204.

19. Michael R. A. Chance, ed., *Social Fabrics of the Mind* (London: Lawrence Erlbaum Associates, 1988), p. 2.

20. Peter Matthiessen, *Under the Mountain Wall* (London: Heinemann, 1963), p. 7.

21. A. S. Einarsen, "Some Factors Affecting Ring-necked

Pheasant Population Density" (1945), *Murrelet* 26:39–44. Cited in Robert Hinde, *Ethology* (London: Collins/Fontana, 1982), p. 142.

22. J. B. Calhoun, "Population Density and Social Pathology" (1962), *Scientific American* 206:139–48.

23. Solly Zuckerman, *The Social Life of Monkeys and Apes* (London: Kegan Paul, Trench, Trubner, 1932).

24. Adolph H. Schultz, *The Life of Primates* (London: Weidenfeld & Nicolson, 1969), pp. 239–40.

## 2. *Aggressive Personality Disorders*

1. James Shields, "Genetics and Mental Development," in Michael Rutter, ed., *Scientific Foundations of Developmental Psychiatry* (London: Heinemann Medical Books, 1980), pp. 15–16.

2. Hans J. Eysenck, *Crime and Personality* (London: Routledge & Kegan Paul, 1964), p. 62.

3. Leon Radzinowicz and Joan King, *The Growth of Crime* (London: Hamish Hamilton, 1977), pp. 92–93.

4. Nicholas N. Kittrie, *The Right to Be Different* (Baltimore: Johns Hopkins Press, 1971), p. 265.

5. William Alwyn Lishman, *Organic Psychiatry* (Oxford: Blackwell Scientific Publications, 1978), p. 634.

6. Luigi Valzelli, "Aggression and Violence: A Biological Essay of the Distinction," in L. Valzelli and L. Morgese, eds., *Aggression and Violence: A Psycho/Biological and Clinical Approach* (Milan: Edizioni Saint Vincent, 1981), pp. 48–49.

7. Lishman, p. 104.

8. J. R. Stevens and V. Milstein, "Severe Psychiatric Disorders of Childhood: Electroencephalogram and Clinical Correlations" (1970), *American Journal of Diseases of Children* 120:182–92.

9. Leonard Berkowitz, *Aggression: A Social Psychological Analysis* (New York: McGraw-Hill, 1962), p. 291.

10. D. P. Farrington, "The Family Backgrounds of Aggressive Youths," in L. A. Hersov, M. Berger, and D. Shaffer, eds., *Aggression and Anti-Social Behaviour in Childhood and Adolescence* (Oxford: Pergamon Press, 1978), pp. 73–74.

11. Michael Rutter, *Maternal Deprivation Reassessed* (Harmondsworth: Penguin, 1981), pp. 179–98.

12. Tony Parker, *The Frying Pan* (London: Hutchinson, 1970), pp. 84, 86.

13. Tony Parker and Robert Allerton, *The Courage of His Convictions* (London: Hutchinson, 1962), p. 34.

14. Muriel Gardiner, *The Deadly Innocents: Portraits of Children Who Kill* (London: Hogarth Press, 1977), pp. 95–128.

15. John R. Hamilton, "Identification of High Risk Groups," in *Helping Victims of Violence* (The Hague: Ministry of Welfare, Health and Cultural Affairs, Government Publishing Office, 1983), pp. 116–17.

16. Kevin Howells, "Social Relationshps in Violent Offenders," in S. Duck and R. Gilmour, eds., *Personal Relationships in Disorder* (London: Academic Press, 1981), pp. 219–20.

17. Ibid., pp. 216–17.

18. Kittrie, p. 193.

19. Jonas Robitscher, *The Powers of Psychiatry* (Boston: Houghton Mifflin, 1980), pp. 151–52.

20. Tony Whitehead, *Mental Illness and the Law* (Oxford: Basil Blackwell, 1983), pp. 125–26.

21. Norval Morris and Gordon Hawkins, *The Honest Politician's Guide to Crime Control* (Chicago: University of Chicago Press, 1970), p. 179.

## 3. *Sadomasochism*

1. Hans J. Eysenck and Glenn Wilson, *The Psychology of Sex* (London: Dent, 1979), p. 79.

2. Clellan S. Ford and Frank A. Beach, *Patterns of Sexual Behaviour* (London: Methuen, 1965), pp. 60–61.

3. Melvin Konner, *The Tangled Wing* (New York: Holt, Rinehart & Winston, 1982), pp. 289–90.

4. Alfred C. Kinsey, Wardell B. Pomeroy, Clyde E. Martin, and Paul H. Gebhard, *Sexual Behavior in the Human Female* (Philadelphia: Saunders, 1953), pp. 704–5.

5. Karl Berg, *The Sadist* (London: Acorn Press, 1938).

6. Ludovic Kennedy, *10 Rillington Place* (London: Gollancz, 1961).

7. E. Williams, *Beyond Belief* (London: Hamish Hamilton, 1967).

8. Paul H. Gebhard, John H. Gagnon, Wardell B. Pomeroy, and Cornelia V. Christenson, *Sex Offenders* (London: Heinemann, 1965), p. 134.

9. Gordon Burn, ''. . . *somebody's Husband, somebody's Son*'' (London: Heinemann, 1984).

10. Brian Masters, *Killing for Company* (London: Cape, 1985).

11. Robert P. Brittain, "The Sadistic Murderer" (1970): *Medicine, Science and the Law* 10:198–207.

12. A. N. Groth, *Men Who Rape* (New York: Plenum, 1979).

13. Frans B. M. de Waal, "The Reconciled Hierarchy," in M. R. A. Chance, ed., *Social Fabrics of the Mind* (Hove: Lawrence Erlbaum, 1988), p. 131.

14. Roger Brown, *Social Psychology* (New York: Free Press, 1965), p. 74.

15. Abraham H. Maslow, H. Rand, and S. Newman, "Some Parallels between Sexual and Dominance Behaviour of Infrahuman Primates and the Fantasies of Patients in Psychotherapy," in Maslow, ed., *The Farther Reaches of Human Nature* (Harmondsworth: Penguin, 1973), pp. 369–86.

16. Michael R. A. Chance and Clifford J. Jolly, *Social Groups of Monkeys, Apes and Men* (New York: Dutton, 1970), p. 187.

17. De Waal, p. 114.

18. Sigmund Freud, *The Interpretation of Dreams*, Standard Edition, vol. 5 (London: Hogarth Press, 1958), p. 354.

19. J. W. Mohr, R. E. Turner, and M. B. Jerry, *Pedophilia and Exhibitionism* (Toronto: University of Toronto Press, 1964), p. 164.

20. George Painter, *Marcel Proust*, vol. 2 (London: Chatto & Windus, 1965), pp. 262–70.

21. Quoted in Philip Henderson, *Swinburne* (New York: Macmillan, 1974), p. 131.

22. Quoted in Gilles Deleuze, *Sacher-Masoch*, trans. Jean McNeil (London: Faber, 1971), p. 231.

23. Simone de Beauvoir, *The Marquis de Sade*, trans. Paul Dinnage (London: Calder, 1962), pp. 45–46.

24. Angus Wilson, *The Strange Ride of Rudyard Kipling* (London: Secker & Warburg, 1977), p. 50.

25. Kinsey et al., p. 677.

26. Gebhard et al., p. 669.

27. Beatrice Faust, *Women, Sex, and Pornography* (Harmondsworth: Penguin, 1981), p. 48.

28. Kinsey et al., p. 687.

29. Chris Gosselin and Glenn Wilson, "Fetishism and Sadomasochism," in Howells, ed., *The Psychology of Sexual Diversity* (Oxford: Blackwell, 1986), pp. 91–92.

30. Ibid., p. 93.

31. Private communication, quoted with permission.

32. Quoted in Gilbert Lely, *The Marquis de Sade*, trans. Alec Brown (London: Elek, 1961), p. 25.

33. *Report of the Committee on Obscenity and Film Censorship*, Chairman, Bernard Williams (London: Her Majesty's Stationery Office, 1979), p. 108.

34. Steven Marcus, *The Other Victorians* (London: Weidenfeld & Nicolson, 1966), p. 282.

35. John Cleland, *Fanny Hill* (London: Mayflower, 1963), pp. 175–83.

36. Pauline Réage, *Histoire d'O* (Paris: Jean-Jacques Pauvert, 1962).

37. Otto Fenichel, *The Psychoanalytic Theory of Neurosis* (New York: Norton, 1945), p. 231.

38. Marcus, p. 263.

39. Sigmund Freud, *Three Essays on the Theory of Sexuality*, Standard Edition, vol. 7 (London: Hogarth Press, 1953), pp. 157–58.

40. Karen Horney, "On the Genesis of the Castration Complex in Women," in *Feminine Psychology* (New York: Norton, 1967), p. 38.

41. John E. Mack, *A Prince of Our Disorder* (London: Weidenfeld & Nicolson, 1976), pp. 415–41.

## 4. *The Ubiquity of Paranoia*

1. Lewis F. Richardson, *Statistics of Deadly Quarrels* (London: Stevens & Sons, 1960), p. 153.

2. Kevin Browne, "Family Violence and Child Abuse," in John Archer and Kevin Browne, eds., *Human Aggression: Naturalistic Approaches* (London: Routledge, 1989), p. 190.

3. Ibid., p. 185.

4. B. F. Steele and C. B. Pollack, "A Psychiatric Study of Parents Who Abuse Infants and Small Children," in R. E. Helfer and C. H. Kempe, eds., *The Battered Child*, 2d ed. (Chicago: University of Chicago Press, 1968).

5. *The Independent*, November 22, 1989, p. 3.

6. Stanley Milgram, *Obedience to Authority* (New York: Harper and Row, 1974), p. 3.

7. Ibid., p. 8.

8. Ibid.

9. Hannah Arendt, *Eichmann in Jerusalem: A Report on the Banality of Evil* (New York: Viking Press, 1963).

10. Bruno Bettelheim, *Surviving and Other Essays* (New York: Knopf, 1979), pp. 270–71.

11. Milgram, p. 188.

12. Konrad Lorenz, *On Aggression* (London: Methuen, 1966), p. 207.

13. Ibid., p. 208.

14. Roger Brown, *Social Psychology*, 2d ed. (New York: Free Press, 1986), p. 589.

15. Ibid., p. 590.

16. George Orwell, *Animal Farm* (Harmondsworth: Penguin, 1951), p. 114.

17. Brown, p. 534.

18. Roger Brown, *Social Psychology* (New York: Free Press, 1965), p. 750.

19. Quoted in Surajit Sinha, "Caste in India: Its Essential Pattern of Socio-Cultural Integration," in Anthony de Rueck and Julie Knight, eds., *Caste and Race* (London: J. & A. Churchill, 1967), p. 103.

20. Hiroshi Wagatsuma, "The Pariah Caste in Japan: History and Present Self-Image," in de Reuck and Knight, eds., pp. 118–19.

21. Ibid., p. 120.

22. Norman Cohn, *Europe's Inner Demons* (New York: Basic Books, 1975), p. xi.

23. Heinrich Kramer and James Sprenger, *Malleus Maleficarum*, translated and edited by the Rev. Montague Summers (London: Pushkin Press, 1948), p. 47.

24. Ibid., p. 58.

25. Ibid., p. xvi.

26. Cohn, p. 253.

27. Norman Cohn, *Warrant for Genocide* (London: Eyre & Spottiswoode, 1967), p. 252.

28. Quoted in Cohn, *Warrant for Genocide*, pp. 152–53.

29. Quoted in Nicholas Mosley, *Beyond the Pale* (London: Secker & Warburg, 1983), p. 96.

30. Nicholas Goodricke-Clarke, *The Occult Roots of Nazism* (Wellingborough: Aquarian Press, 1985), p. 203.

31. Ibid.

32. Quoted in Gitta Sereny, *Into That Darkness* (New York: McGraw-Hill, 1974), p. 101.

33. Anthony Storr, *Solitude* (New York: Free Press, 1988; London: Collins, 1989).

34. Francisco Goya, epigraph to *Los Caprichos* (New York: Dover, 1970).

35. Revelation 21:1–4.

36. Revelation 20:12–15.

5. *"What Is to Be Done?"*

1. Isaiah Berlin, *Russian Thinkers* (London: Hogarth Press, 1978), p. 228.

2. Jerome Kagan, *The Nature of the Child* (New York: Basic Books, 1984), p. 39.

3. Ibid., p. 100.

4. Ibid., p. 71.

5. Richard de Boer, private communication.

6. Ibid.

7. Paul Sieghart, *The Lawful Rights of Mankind* (Oxford: Oxford University Press, 1985), pp. 113—14.

8. *The Handbook of Medical Ethics* (London: British Medical Association, 1984), sections 6.15, 6.16., p. 44.

9. Anthony Storr, *Churchill's Black Dog, Kafka's Mice, and Other Phenomena of the Human Mind* (New York: Grove Weidenfeld, 1988; London: Collins, 1989), pp. 303—7.

10. Norval Morris and Gordon Hawkins, *The Honest Politician's Guide to Crime Control* (Chicago: University of Chicago Press, 1970), p. 83.

# Index

175

# About the Author

Anthony Storr, the internationally acclaimed author of such groundbreaking works as *The Art of Psychotherapy* and *The Essential Jung*, is Honorary Consulting Psychiatrist to the Oxfordshire Health Authority and Emeritus Fellow of Green College, Oxford. He is also a Fellow of the Royal College of Physicians, a Fellow of the Royal College of Psychiatrists, and a Fellow of the Royal Society of Literature.